CW00507717

THE DROITWICH CANALS
Navigation Guide and Visitor Guide
First edition 2011

Compiled by Margaret Rowley and Robin Smithett,
with the welcome assistance of Mick Yarker, Geoff Trevis, Roger Claxton and Derek Nash.
Particular thanks are due to Jason Leach of British Waterways.

The authors gratefully acknowledge the assistance of Wychavon District Council and the Droitwich Spa
Area Partnership in the production of this volume.

Published by

DROITWICH CANALS TRUST LIMITED
Registered office: Island House, Moor Road, Chesham HP5 1NZ
Registered charity number: 266515.
2011

All photos and graphics by Robin Smithett unless otherwise credited.

Artwork & Printing by Free Range Design & Print Solutions, Bedford.

ISBN: 978-0-9568183-0-0

CONTENTS

Hanbury Locks open day, 2008

Salwarpe cutting

FOREWORD

by Max Sinclair, President of Droitwich Canals Trust

In 1959 while working on the Stratford Canal restoration I thought about my local Droitwich waterway, which was abandoned in 1939, and realised that restoration was feasible.

Writing letters to local newspapers and Councils, I gradually gained support from fellow enthusiasts in the then Worcester Birmingham Canal Society and importantly from the Architect and Chief Engineer for the Droitwich New Town development.

Over the years hundreds of dedicated volunteers came to the canal and worked, often in dreadful mud and dangerous conditions, to clear some 300,000 tons of spoil from the channel and rebuild the frost damaged lock walls.

We now have the satisfaction of seeing this historically important canal coming alive and providing a major amenity to boaters, walkers and cyclists while admiring the pioneering work of the great canal engineer James Brindley.

I trust this guide book will enable many more people to appreciate all that the restored Canal has to offer.

A photo from 1890 of James Brindley's original bridge taking the Barge Canal under what is now the A449. This bridge is now hidden alongside the new canal tunnel. (from the collection of Max Sinclair).

INTRODUCTION

This book is designed as a guide for visitors to the newly re-opened Droitwich Canals. It is intended for boaters, walkers and anyone visiting the canals.

It deals briefly with the history of the area and of the Canals, as well as their restoration.

There is a step by step navigation guide with detailed maps, as well as a visitor guide to points of interest along the route.

There are notes on wildlife to be found along the canal at different times of the year.

For those wanting to explore on foot, there are a series of walks beside and around the canal.

For boaters, there is a list of essential services on the canal, and a guide to the Mid-Worcestershire cruising ring created by the re-opening of the Droitwich Canals.

This first edition of the Guide has been written to coincide with the re-opening of the Canals. There will inevitably be some minor changes to the navigational aspects once boats start to use the Canals, and for the latest information we recommend consulting www.waterscape.com/things-to-do/boating/guides.

Welcome sign at Hawford Lock 2

THE FUTURE

The future of the Droitwich Canals is now brighter than it has been for the past century. The re-opening has brought both canals back to life.

The re-opening will bring benefits to many people who live or work by the canals, and will bring many people to the canals who have never visited before.

The improvements to the environment of the canals will bring pleasure to those who walk, cycle or cruise them, and the local economy will be uplifted.

The opening of the Mid Worcestershire cruising Ring will help to gain popularity for the Droitwich Canals, but publicity will have to be maintained to ensure the momentum of this exciting development is not lost.

With restoration having been ongoing since 1973, the two waterways have been restored to a high standard. However, the re-opening is not the end of the task.

Custody of the waterways is expected to move into the third sector, which means that more of the work to care for them will have to be carried out by volunteers.

Although the canals will be fully re-opened, improvements may still be desirable or required.

A SHORT HISTORY OF DROITWICH

Note: a great deal more information about the history of Droitwich, its canals and their early restoration may be found in the Droitwich Canals Trust's book 'The Illustrated Droitwich Canal Guide'.

Droitwich is a town literally built on salt. Since ancient times, salt has been valued as a preservative for food as well as for curing hides and healing wounds.

Droitwich sits on massive brine deposits and salt was originally produced here in pre-historic times. The Romans called the town Salinae. In the 5th century, the Romans left and later the Anglo Saxons had salt furnaces here. The borough of Droitwich was England's major salt producing centre and is the most frequently mentioned place in the Domesday Book.

Brine rose naturally to the surface under sub-artesian pressure at three sites along the River Salwarpe in what is now Vines Park in the centre of Droitwich. This brine was unusually fully saturated, and was extremely valuable because it was economic to boil, and the yield of salt was high. The brine was evaporated over wood or later coal fires, to which the soot-blackened church overlooking Vines Park bears witness.

In the 18th century it was found that bore-holes could be sunk to reach brine in unlimited quantities without having to rely on natural brine flow. With this increase in production and later pumping to draw the brine, there was gradual subsidence in some parts of the town.

John Corbett was a leading personality in the history of Droitwich in the 19th century. He invested in the salt industry and in later years became known as the "Salt King".

He built a magnificent house, completed in 1875, in the style of Louis XIII. The house is now the Chateau Impney Hotel and stands as a landmark to anyone entering the town from the North.

With the decline of the salt industry in the late 19th century (due to the use of ice and later refrigeration, better salt wells elsewhere and subsidence), John Corbett became interested in developing the town as a Spa.

The potential first became apparent in 1823 during a cholera epidemic. There was no water, so sick people were advised to bathe in hot brine. People recovered from their illnesses miraculously and the benefits of bathing in brine were discovered.

Droitwich Spa retains its reputation as a Spa town with other facilities including a modern sports centre and an open-air lido.

References:

Squires, Roger W (1984): A Guide to the Droitwich Canals: Droitwich Canals Trust

Axe, Jon and Sinclair, Max (2001): The Illustrated Droitwich Canals Guide: Droitwich Canals Trust

Blewitt, Lyn and Field, Bob (1994): Droitwich: A Pictorial History: Phillimore and Co.

Middlemass, Barbara (2009): The Chateau at Impney: Saltway Press

A SHORT HISTORY OF THE DROITWICH CANALS

The Romans canalised the River Salwarpe to get the salt from Droitwich to other settlements. With flooding in the winter and low water in the summer the river was not always reliable. In 1762 the great canal builder James Brindley met with the salt producers to plan a canal from Droitwich to the River Severn. The enabling Act was passed in 1768 and the canal was completed in 1771.

In the 18th century, salt production increased considerably with the demand for salt to preserve food for the industrial cities. Salt brought down the canal to the Severn then went to Gloucester by way of the river and overland to the Thames, or to Bristol. The canal was also used to bring coal into Droitwich for the salt production.

Boats were towed from the bank by teams of men before there was a towing path. This was introduced in 1806, when horses replaced men for towing. To coincide with the opening of the Junction Canal, the Barge Canal locks were lengthened to accommodate standard length narrowboats.

The railway came to Droitwich in 1852 and took most of the trade. At about the same time, John Corbett concentrated his salt production at Stoke Prior, further reducing Droitwich's trade.

The Junction Canal was one of the last canals to be built in 1854, and was constructed in a vain attempt to counter the threat of railway competition. The side ponds by the Hanbury locks were to limit the amount of water taken from the Worcester & Birmingham Canal.

The last use of the Barge Canal was in 1916, and the last boat on the Junction Canal left in 1929. The canals were legally abandoned in 1939.

The 1960s saw the rebuilding of a railway bridge in Droitwich, but by this time there were those who had ideas of restoring the canal, so this was not culverted as proposed.

At the same time, when the M5 motorway was being built, thousands of tons of spoil were dumped in the canal basin. The M5 itself almost succeeded in cutting the canal in half, but luckily the culvert to take the Body Brook was modified in the 1990s (when the motorway was widened) to be just large enough to allow the passage of boats.

St Richard's House, Victoria Square which was the site of the St. Andrew's Brine Baths. It now houses the Tourist Information Centre, Salt Museum and Town Council Offices. Photograph courtesy of Droitwich Spa Town Council.

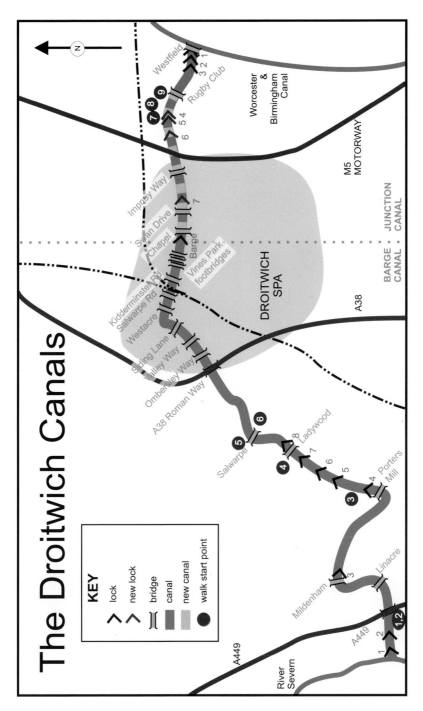

The Droitwich Canals

KEY

⋋	lock
⋋	new lock
]⋵	bridge
	canal
	new canal
●	walk start point

Westfield Rd
Rugby Club
3 2 1
3
9 8 7
5 4
6

Worcester & Birmingham Canal

M5 MOTORWAY

Impney Way
Swan Drive
Chapel
7
Barge
Vines Park footbridges
Kidderminster Rd
Salwarpe Rd
Westacre
Siding Lane
Valley Way
Ombersley Way
A38 Roman Way

DROITWICH SPA

A38

BARGE · JUNCTION
CANAL · CANAL

6
Ladywood
8
5
7
4
6
Salwarpe
5
3
4 Porters Mill

Mildenham
3
Linacre

A449
2
1,2
1

A449

River Severn

THE RESTORATION OF THE DROITWICH CANALS

After initial moves to at least prevent further deterioration in the 1960s, and some work by volunteers, the Droitwich Canals Trust was formed in 1973, the local authority having the freehold and granting the Canal Trust a 99 year lease on the canals. Over the next decades, volunteer workers from the Trust, the Waterway Recovery Group and hundreds of community workers of all kinds laboured to retain the canals as a living museum. They cleared towpaths and trees, dredged the canal and fitted new lock gates. Without this work, the full restoration could never have been conceived.

Over one weekend in the 1970s, the 'Big Dig' attracted more than 1000 restoration volunteers. The summit level of the Barge canal was in many places just a damp depression in the fields.

However, there were several huge challenges to complete restoration as a navigable waterway which could not be overcome with volunteer effort and charitable donations alone.

Widespread public support for the restoration and recognition of the benefits that restoration would bring led to the formation of the Droitwich Canals Restoration Partnership in 2001.

Lock 1 at Hawford prior to restoration in 2005

The first boat through Lock 1, Hawford after restoration. 6th September 2010

Lock 2 at Hawford prior to restoration in 2005

Lock 2 at Hawford in restored condition

Droitwich Canals Trust joined with British Waterways, The Waterways Trust, Worcestershire County Council and Wychavon District Council to restore the canals to working order, with British Waterways project managing the construction works.

On the Barge Canal, work still required to be done: silt removal from locks, a great deal of dredging, removal of undergrowth, new lock gates, lock walls rebuilt and installing mooring pontoons. One of the major pieces of work required was to tunnel under the A449 dual carriageway. On the Junction Canal, complete new sections of canal had to be dug in order to utilise the motorway culvert. New locks also had to be built and a section of the River Salwarpe canalised.

The A449 tunnel under construction in 2009

The culvert under A449 dual carriageway

The A449 tunnel nearing competion

The first boat passes through the A449 tunnel

In total, the project restored nearly 8 miles of waterway linking Droitwich to the River Severn at Hawford and the Worcester & Birmingham Canal at Hanbury. This included the restoration of 12 existing locks and the construction of 4 new locks, the digging of 1km of new canal & 500m of canalised river.

In addition to work on the canals themselves, the project involved the creation of an offline reedbed (at Coney Meadow) to replace the reeds removed from the channel. The restoration will also provide education resources, volunteering and training opportunities, circular walks and improved access to the towpath.

The total cost of the restoration was over £11m, with major contributions from The Heritage Lottery Fund, Advantage West Midlands (the former Regional Development Agency), Worcestershire County Council, Wychavon District Council and British Waterways. Other funders have contributed to specific aspects of the restoration, as well as local appeals.

The stretch below Lock 3 at Mildenham prior to restoration

A cruiser approaches Lock 3 at Mildenham

Porters Mill Lock prior to restoration

First boat prepares to leave Porters Mill Lock

The benefits of the restoration will not just be for the thousands of walkers, boaters, cyclists, anglers and canoeists that can enjoy the canal, but Droitwich and the surrounding area will benefit from increased visitor numbers and investment.

For more details of the early days of restoration, see the Droitwich Canals Trust's book 'The Illustrated Droitwich Canal Guide'.

The completed staircase locks 4 and 5

The staircase locks take shape in concrete in 2008

A new length of canal below the Rugby Club bridge before watering

The brand new bridge carrying the Droitwich Rugby Club Road over the Junction Canal

VISITOR GUIDE

This section describes the features on or adjacent to the Droitwich Canals, and is arranged from Hawford on the River Severn to Hanbury Junction on the Worcester & Birmingham Canal, running roughly south west to north east.

At various points along the canals, there are a series of wooden posts set in the towpath, with mosaic panels inset into them. These are Audio Trail markers, and are shown on the maps in this book as small numbered red squares. The audio trail narrative can be downloaded from www.waterscape.com/droitwich.

HAWFORD TO MILDENHAM (see map on page 26)

The Droitwich Canals run parallel to the River Salwarpe for approximately six miles of their seven and a half mile length. The River Salwarpe was used to take salt from Droitwich to the Severn and on to Sharpness for export. It also brought coal in the reverse direction. The Saxon name for the river - Sal (salt) and Warpe (boat haulage) - suggests navigation was possible at that time. In 1378 Richard II granted the bailiffs of Droitwich the right to levy tolls on the river, but by 1600 the river was no longer navigable. Some attempts were made to re-open the Salwarpe to navigation, and it was still used to a limited extent until the Droitwich Barge canal was planned in 1768.

Tales are told of a Wych barge, possibly the 'Volunteer', being sunk in the River Severn across the mouth of Hawford Lock in 1939. Special excavation works were carried out during the final restoration of the Canal but no trace of a sunken barge was found.

Just before the A 449 tunnel you will see to the south a fine Georgian building which is the Kings Hawford school, the junior school of the independent Kings School in Worcester.

The new tunnel constructed to take the canal under the A449 is an uncompromising concrete structure, in stark contrast to the original picturesque Brindley bridge (see page 4). During the second world war, the old bridge was considered to be too weak to take the tank transporters that were coming down from Liverpool and it was in-filled with concrete by Italian prisoners of war in 1942. A small tunnel and four tubes were inserted to take the remaining canal water. The road was later made into a dual carriageway in the 1960s and the bridge was buried. There was no engineering drawing of the position of the old bridge, and this caused problems when the new tunnel was built, since it was important not to disturb the structure.

The River Salwarpe had been a possible alternative route for the canal restoration from the River Severn, avoiding the need for the tunnel, but would have required new locks and straightening of the River Salwarpe. Fortunately this was avoided and the original line of the canal was restored instead.

There are a number of mills along the River Salwarpe. Hawford Mill, which was possibly built on the site of Hawford Old Mill, was referred to in 1659, destroyed in 1767 and rebuilt in 1815. Corn was last ground here in 1910. Remains of the mill can be seen in the grounds of the George Judge boat yard adjacent to the A449. The boat yard also houses a holiday site of permanent caravans, camping ground and cafe. Beyond the boat yard are some fishing lakes.

To access the towpath from the A449, park in the lay-by just past the bridge over the canal on the north bound carriageway. There is a footpath from Lock 1 that runs alongside the River Severn from Lock Lane, Hawford all the way to Worcester.

Linacre Bridge (Bridge 3) has served as a farm accommodation bridge since the canal was constructed.

A listed structure, it is the only bridge that has remained virtually unaltered since the canal was first built. Its red bricks and sandstone trimmers are in quite good repair, but show deep rope grooves from early use by the Wych barges.

The narrow Egg Lane leads to Mildenham Mill from the A449 and crosses the canal on bridge 4, which is a Brindley designed lock tail bridge. The lock at this point was partially restored many years ago and the volunteers were astonished to find that a number of safes had been dumped in the water. Dumping heavy objects in the canal has always presented the volunteers with a major headache, so posts have been erected on what has become a parking area at the south side of the lock to try to prevent this in future.

Mildenham Mill was operated by Bill Watts until 1946 and was known locally as Bill's Mill. The mill was restored to working order by Denis Watts in 1970, but it is now a private residence. There has been a mill on the site for over 1000 years and parts of the present structure date from 1609, although the rectangular mill building is 18th century. The mill buildings can be viewed from the public footpath to the east of the mill grounds.

PORTERS MILL TO LADYWOOD (see map on page 28)

The half-timbered Manor House immediately to the west of the canal just before Porters Mill Bridge (Bridge 5) was built in 1503. One of the Manor's owners was the Mace Bearer for Queen Elizabeth I. A royal coat of arms decorates one of the main fireplaces. The house was badly damaged in the devastating flood of July 2007 but has been extensively renovated.

Porters Mill Bridge itself is of Brindley design and the sandstone blocks on the parapet still show rope grooves.

Further up the lane on the River Salwarpe is John Porter's Mill. There have been mills on this site since the Norman Conquest. The present mill dates from 1881.

A public footpath leads from Porters Mill bridge to the large village of Fernhill Heath (some 2 miles away) which has a general store, hairdresser's shop and two pubs. This footpath forms part of the Monarch's Way long distance footpath which follows the route taken by King Charles II in his escape from Cromwell after being defeated in the final battle of the Civil War at Worcester in 1651. The Monarch's Way continues along the canal towpath up to Siding Lane Bridge, where it turns north to Westwood Park and Hampton Lovett.

Parking at Porters Mill is alongside the road just past Porters Mill Lock Cottage. This stretch of canal is very popular with fishermen, and there is often little space available.

National Cycle Route 46 comes down from Claines and follows the road across Bridge 5 and past Lock 4 continuing along the road to cross back over Bridge 6 at Ladywood.

In between are the Ladywood flight of locks. The Martin Brook flows alongside the canal for a distance before passing under it above

Porters Mill

15

A trip to Ladywood

Lock 6: then the canal curves along the shallow valley of the brook. If you cross the lock gates at Lock 6, you can inspect the reconstructed Brindley circular weir. It was built with new materials in the 70s on the site of the original which was discovered during lock clearance. Brindley used the Droitwich Canal to try out different new ideas. These round spill weirs later became a feature of his Staffs and Worcs Canal.

Lock 8 is situated by Ladywood Lock Cottage. This is the last lock until the canal joins the River Salwarpe in Droitwich Spa. Ladywood Lock Cottage was renovated by Droitwich Canals Trust in 1981 and was used as a base for the Trust during the early restoration work.

The locks on the Barge Canal were originally built by Brindley to a length of 64 feet to accommodate the Wych (or Wich) Barges taking salt from Droitwich and returning with coal and other essentials. Like all the other locks on the Barge Canal it was lengthened to accommodate the later 'standard' 70ft narrow boats. A hundred years ago loaded Wych Barges with a make-weight boat in tow would be hauled along by a horse on their way to the River Severn, where the make-weight load was added, and then on by sail to far flung destinations such as France! Funny to think Droitwich was an inland port for France.

LADYWOOD TO CHAWSON (see map on page 30)

The Canal passes through a number of cuttings along this section which has some pleasantly wooded sides. The canal has now moved away from the Salwarpe valley in which is sited the New Mill, a working mill until 1828.

Once the canal swings to the right there are good views opening up to the left. When the canal was built, Brindley was concerned that in the event of a breach on this long embankment the escaping water would rush through and tear down a great section, draining the whole canal between Vines Park and Ladywood Lock. To reduce the potential damage he fitted special gates in the bed of the canal which would raise if there was a breach. The gates were hinged at the bottom and the pressure of the water remaining in the canal would keep them tightly sealed. In fact a breach never took place and it was only when the volunteers excavated the cutting at Salwarpe that a gate, still intact, was rediscovered!

As you walk the embankment section keep an eye out for the old swing bridge that has been placed to the left of the towpath. You will see that the canal is narrow here where the bridge once went across, carrying a private path to Hill End Farm House. Access across the canal is no longer required, so the bridge, which was in poor condition, was removed. It is much narrower than its counterparts in Vines Park and mainly constructed of wood. The story goes that Brindley designed the swing bridges on the Barge Canal and the bearings they revolved upon were made from cannon balls running in races. This was said to be the first recorded use of ball bearings! The bridge has been left for the time being as an item of display. The wide space on the towpath has had a picnic bench installed by volunteers.

Salwarpe Church   –

The canal has two sharp bends either side of Salwarpe village because the Canal Act prevented the canal from passing to the west of the church - to protect Salwarpe Mill. The bridge, numbered 7, is in red brick with high level scaffold bearers beneath the arch with hardwood padstones. At the end of the cutting, a short steep footpath leads off the towpath to the 12th century Church of St Michael and All Angels with its magnificent tower.

If you take a right turn when entering the churchyard and walk round the back of the church, in the hedge is a big cast iron cauldron with ivy growing over it. This is reputed to date back to the construction of the canal and was used for purposes unknown by the canal builders. I would say it is far too big for melting lead (one theory), but sure to have been used for a process involving heat. Any guesses?

Just beyond the cauldron is a flight of 48 moss-covered stone steps leading down to the site of the old mill leat, which is now dry. A plank bridge takes the path to the old mill dam. This is the only remaining feature of the mill which was demolished in 1942.

Attempts at making the river navigable had been tried right back to Roman times. In the 15th century, this included the installation of flash locks, one of which is thought to have been here. The locks had a single gate, which was removed to allow a boat to pass, then replaced.

The green to the other side of the canal bridge had a whipping post and stocks until the 1850s. The village has a spacious village hall, which is the centre for a large summer fete held each year.

The Copcut Elm is a large public house about a mile away on the corner of Copcut Lane and the Worcester Road, and serves meals. There is a footpath all along the narrow road to it.

Churchfields Farm is famous for its home made ice cream which is sold locally at the Brookside Fruits Farm shop about half a mile from the Copcut Elm in the Worcester direction along the A38 Worcester Road.

Salwarpe Court can be seen towering over the canal half way along Salwarpe cutting on the East side. It was built in early Tudor times by Sir John Talbot. The Talbot family continued in residence until 1780. The original timber framing is close studded with herringbone brick in-filling of a later date except for the solar side where the bay has an upper overhang with carved barge-board decoration.

A new reed bed has been constructed between the canal and the River Salwarpe at Coney Meadow. There is access to a hide and a footpath through part of the nature reserve parallel to the towpath. The reeds have been grown from those removed from the canal during the restoration as an alternative nesting site to accommodate the displaced reed buntings and reed warblers.

At the entrance to Coney Meadow is a picnic table and on the opposite bank are the remains of the now disused accommodation bridge to Salwarpe Court. Towards the end of the reed bed site is a fully restored Brindley-designed brick spill weir.

This section abounds with wildlife and it is easy to see why the conservationists were not totally in favour of disturbing the canal in order to restore it. However, this is a totally man-made waterway and left to nature it would silt up and the reed beds would gradually disappear as the bed dried up. The banks of the Salwarpe are perilously close and could breach if unattended, eventually draining the canal completely. Trees would grow through the clay puddle so that it no longer held water, and the whole diverse environment would change. Add man's obsession with dumping and this wonderful scene would become an overgrown rubbish tip. The canal requires continual careful and sensitive maintenance to keep it beautiful and a haven for nature.

CHAWSON VALLEY (see map on page 32)

The Roman Way bridge carries the A38 Droitwich outer ring road across the canal and the River Salwarpe, and marks the town boundary.

The canal now passes playing fields and Droitwich Community Woods to the west, and Chawson Valley housing to the east. Immediately after passing under the next road bridge (Ombersley Way) the Sidings Lane Basin can be seen to the east of the canal. This is still largely filled with reeds.

The town's Leisure Centre is immediately to the west of the canal after Bridge 11. There is a large car park serving the Leisure Centre and nearby playing fields which gives easy access to the canal. The Leisure Centre also includes a café.

DROITWICH SPA (see map on page 34 and Town Plan on page 23)

Vines Park lies at the heart of the history of Droitwich Spa. The Romans grew vines there. A Roman cemetery was excavated in Vines Lane to the north of the park, and beyond that to the north of the Worcester to Bromsgrove railway line is the site of Salinae, a Roman industrial settlement producing salt. There is evidence of Stone Age salt making in the same area. The Church of St Augustine on Dodderhill standing high above the Vines was blackened by the smoke from more recent salt works that grew up around the area. Coal-fired furnaces were used to evaporate the brine which flows under the town and was pumped up through a number of salt pits and piped to several salt works alongside the canal. The canal was originally constructed partly to the south of the current line, roughly under the current Saltway which was built as part of the town development scheme in the 1970s.

Statue of St Richard in Vines Park, Droitwich

Wharves serving the salt works extended into the area now occupied by the car park, and the works themselves in the 19th century occupied much of the space between Vines Lane and the High Street / Friar Lane, and between Kidderminster Road and Chapel Bridge and beyond. A salt pump in working order can be seen on Tower Hill, and the replica Upwich brine pit can be seen by the canal in Vines Park. The remains of a chimney base and vacuum cylinder can also be seen in Gurney's Lane between Waitrose and the High Street.

The canal was filled in shortly after the canals were abandoned in 1939, and the current Saltway was built over the former canal wharf and a bowling green over part of the canal. A new line was excavated by the Droitwich Canals Trust shortly after its formation in 1973. The Netherwich Basin was constructed by the Trust to provide moorings, and these moorings were finally constructed by British Waterways in 2010. The obstruction in the basin is said to be the capping of a brine pit. The Railway Inn is the only true canal side pub on the Barge Canal. On the opposite bank is the site of the old gasworks which has been used as a base for the Canal Trust's operations. It is expected that this area will be extensively redeveloped following the opening of the canals.

The canal joins the River Salwarpe at the Barge Lock which is in its original place horizontally, if not vertically. Extraction of brine from under the town has led to some problems of subsidence. This can be seen in the High Street which was quite level in a photo taken in the early 1860s. The Barge Lock has also suffered from subsidence since its construction in 1853. It was rebuilt some 9 ft higher in 1875 and raised another 5ft in 1903. This structure was re-excavated by the Trust in 1981 and again in 2008 by the Waterway Recovery Group of the Inland Waterways Association following a funding appeal.

Today the town of Droitwich Spa has much to offer visitors. The town blends old and new and is a place of great charm and character. This long association with salt is evident in many of the buildings. The High Street is of particular interest as many of the buildings lean at interesting angles due to brine extraction. The town offers a good choice of shops, two supermarkets, pubs, restaurants and cafes ranging from small independent businesses in the High Street to the modern shopping centre in St. Andrews Square. The Heritage Centre in Victoria Square hosts a Salt Museum along with the Tourist Information Centre. Close to the Heritage Centre are the library, banks, post office, police station and medical centre.

There is also a good range of leisure activities including guided walks and a Farmers' Market on the first Saturday of the month in Victoria Square. The Norbury Theatre in Friar Street stages performances and films throughout the year. The town celebrates its heritage with two annual events - St. Richard's Festival and Salt Day.

Lido Park boasts a children's playground, tennis courts and, in the summer, open air bathing in the Lido Pool. The Lido, which originally opened in the 1930s, uses brine, which is added to the pool water making it the same density as sea water. The facility has undergone extensive refurbishment and offers a heated swimming pool and children's wet play area.

John Corbett, the 'Salt King', having moved the focus of salt production from Droitwich to nearby Stoke Prior in 1852, set about turning Droitwich into a Spa town, exploiting the reputed remedial qualities of the brine which had been discovered during the great cholera epidemic of 1832. The first brine baths were built in 1836, and John Corbett built St Andrew's Brine Baths in 1887. The last brine baths, incorporated into the town's private hospital in 1984, closed in 2009. It is hoped that it will be replaced by a similar facility at a different location.

The Lido, first opened in 1935, was also famous for its salt water and was a popular day out for people from Birmingham and the surrounding area. The facility has recently been refurbished and opens in the summer months.

THE JUNCTION CANAL (see map on page 38)

At the Barge Lock the canal joins the River Salwarpe which has again been made navigable. Chapel Bridge carries the former A38 from Worcester to Bromsgrove. The chapel which gave the bridge its name straddled the bridge with the main road passing through it. The reading desk and pulpit stood on one side and the congregation sat on the other. Although this situation no doubt enlivened services, the chapel was demolished in 1763. On the other side of the bridge the Junction Canal diverged from the River Salwarpe but the original line has not been restored as a number of buildings have been constructed over it. Instead the river has been canalised until the canal separates to the east of Swan Drive bridge. From this point the canal and the river part company, the canal roughly running eastwards parallel to the B4090 (the original Roman Saltway) while the Salwarpe flows down from the north. The original line of the canal between Swan Drive and Impney Way was in places closer to the road than it is now.

The next bridge over the canal is another recent construction on Impney Way. The original bridge is used as a garage in the grounds of Kantara. This bridge was called Corbett's Bridge. John Corbett, the Salt King, built Impney Hall in the style of a chateau for his French bride Anna between 1869 and 1875. A track ran between the B4090 and the chateau along the current Impney Way. Anna would travel along this route in order to worship at the Catholic Church at Hadzor. Chateau Impney is currently a hotel and is well worth a visit. The main entrance is from the A38 Bromsgrove Road.

The culvert constructed to take the Body Brook under the M5 was built just wide enough to take a narrow boat, but there was no room for a towpath, so walkers have to use the Hanbury Road and a track at the other side of the motorway. The Body Brook, like the Salwarpe, flows down from the north. The land surrounding the brook is designated a marshland wildlife site.

Mosaic depicting the history of Drotwich in St Andrews Square

The Junction Canal immediately to the east of the M5 is a completely new construction. Although remnants of the old canal can clearly be seen immediately to the south of the new canal and there are no buildings blocking the route the decision was made not to rejoin the original route until the final section past the Rugby Club access road. The modern concrete locks are a complete contrast to the historic locks at Hanbury Wharf.

Parking is available at the access site at the entrance to the Rugby Club. There are information boards here about the canal and local wildlife, a children's play area and picnic tables.

Crossing over the road, the land rises steeply and the canal rises through a flight of three locks. These locks were restored as far as possible to their original condition by Droitwich Canals Trust using a legacy from Neil Pitts, a Midlands waterway enthusiast who left money to the Inland Waterways Association for canal restoration in the area. The brick side ponds are a way of conserving water by filling the pond when a full lock is emptied and returning the water back into the lock when the lock is next filled. This mechanism has been restored and has been demonstrated at annual open days since the restoration. However, they will not always be working when the canal is brought into general use.

The view from the top of the flight looking across to Dodderhill Church is worth noting. Looking to the south, Hadzor Hall can be seen. Built in 1779, the Hall was purchased by John Galton in 1821 and remained in the family until about 1930, when a Catholic college was established. Factory buildings were constructed in the 1960s for the manufacture of ceramic hobs, the factory owner residing in the Hall. In 2000, the factory buildings were demolished, a small estate constructed and the Hall was once again restored to public gaze, although it remains in private ownership. Hadzor village itself is a conservation area and retains its mediaeval form. Many of its buildings are given names of saints reflecting the Catholic connection. The village has two churches, a former Anglican church in the grounds of the Hall (now used as a garden store) and the Catholic church on Hadzor Lane formerly patronised by Mrs. Corbett.

Across the B4090, the Hanbury Wharf Canal Village has a boat yard, chandlery and cafe and other local businesses. The canal cottages include the former lock keeper's cottage and yard master's lodge. The Eagle and Sun public house on the Worcester & Birmingham Canal is renowned for its economically-priced carvery.

PLACES TO GO, THINGS TO DO

DROITWICH SPA HERITAGE AND TOURIST INFORMATION CENTRE, Victoria Square provides a host of information about things to do and places to visit in Droitwich Spa and the surrounding area. It also houses the Salt Museum and Town Council Offices. Tel : (01905) 774312 or e mail heritage@droitwichspa.gov.uk

Information about the town, its history, shops and restaurants can be found at www. droitwichspa.com

DROITWICH LEISURE CENTRE is located to the west of the town centre, just off the bypass. It offers swimming, sports and a health suite together with a café.

DROITWICH LIDO is located on Worcester Road. Large outdoor heated swimming pool and café.

Details of both can be found at: www. wychavonleisure.co.uk

CHURCH OF THE SACRED HEART
208 Worcester Road

This church is decorated with impressive mosaics made of Venetian glass.

HANBURY HALL (NATIONAL TRUST)
School Road, Hanbury
T: 01527 821214
Elegant 18th century family home. The welcoming William & Mary style house was built in 1701: house, tearoom, gardens and parkland.

HAWFORD DOVECOTE (NATIONAL TRUST)
A half-timbered 16th-century dovecote, which retains many of its orginal nesting boxes.

JINNEY RING CRAFT CENTRE
Hanbury village

Textiles, glassware, sculpture, furniture, pottery, paintings, jewellery and woodwork. Workshops, shop, gallery and restaurant. Falconry centre.

DROITWICH COMMUNITY WOODS
Ombersley Way, Droitwich Nature reserve

NORBURY THEATRE
An amateur company with a theatre in Friar Street. Tel: 01905 770154

www.norburytheatre.co.uk

DROITWICH SPA LIBRARY
Victoria Square
Tel: 01905 797401

WALKING
The towpath throughout the canals provides good walking and is suitable for all ages. Wheelchair access is generally good, although in the rural areas, the towpath can become soft and muddy in wet weather. A number of circular walks are included in this book, which between them cover the whole length of the Droitwich Canals. A way-marked walk from Droitwich Leisure Centre round the Coney Meadow Reed Bed is easy walking for all ages and abilities.

ANGLING
The Droitwich Canals offer a great location for fishing. Chub, Roach and Rudd can be found, along with many other species. An Environment Agency Rod Licence is required.
The fishing rights to most lengths of the canals are leased by various local angling clubs, whose names are posted at access points. Some are for members only, but day permits are available, for example on the Ladywood Locks section (locks 5 to 8) from Riflemans AC. Also, in the west end of Droitwich, the Railway Inn AC issues permits. For more information on angling on the canals, see www.waterscape.com

CYCLING
The towpath of the canals is available for cycling throughout. National Cycle routes 45 and 46 follow the canal for part of their length. Cyclists need to respect other towpath users and give way to walkers and other users. Speed should be kept down, and cyclists should dismount under low bridges or where the towpath is narrow. (see www.waterscape.com/things-to-do/cycling)

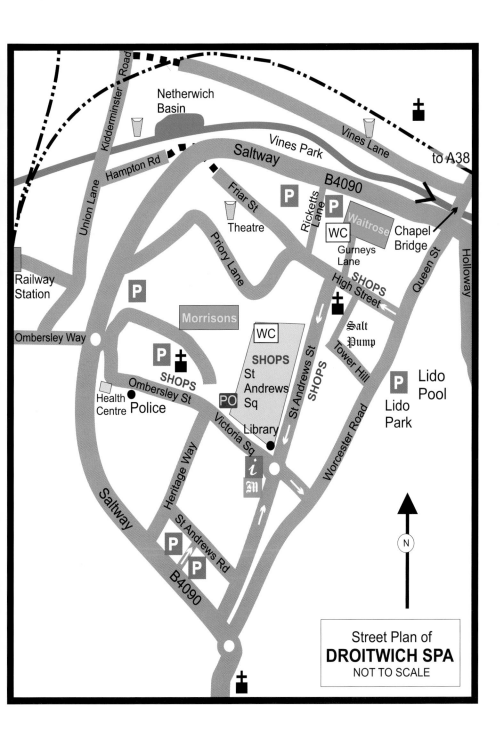

Street Plan of
DROITWICH SPA
NOT TO SCALE

KEY TO MAPS

⩘	lock	P	parking
8	bollards	46	national cycle route
▮	water level warning board	⦶	picnic site
⑥	mileage from Hawford	■ 17	audio trail mosaic post
🚲	cycle track	I	interpretation board

NAVIGATION NOTES - GENERAL

CRAFT DIMENSIONS

BARGE CANAL

Beam: 14ft 6ins (4.4m) up to Bridge 15.

Broad beam length: 61ft (18.8m) - limited by winding hole east of Bridge 13.

Narrow boat length: 71ft 6ins (21.8m).

Constraint point - restricted width: 7ft (2.1m) at Bridge 15. Keep to towpath side

Constraint points - restricted draft at swing bridge sites between A38 and Lock 8: 3ft 6ins (1.1m)

JUNCTION CANAL

Beam: 7ft (2.1m)

Length: 71ft 6ins (21.8m)

Constraint point - headroom in M5 culvert: 6ft 5ins (1.97m)

N.B. Since this is effectively a new navigation, these figures may be subject to change. For the latest information go to www.waterscape.com/things-to-do/boating/guides.

Along most of the length of the Barge Canal, reeds have been retained on both banks of the canal to protect the wildlife. This can make getting a boat into the bank difficult on this stretch. In case of emergency, look for one of the small fishing clearings in the reeds on the towpath side.

Hazards to navigation are shown on the following maps in red. In particular, it must be noted that three natural waterways are associated with the Droitwich Canals: the Severn, the Salwarpe and the Body Brook. Warning boards are located at relevant locks. If the water level on these boards is in the amber sector, navigate with care, as river levels may be rising. If the water level is in the red sector, navigation should not be attempted.

Many of the structures on the canals, and in particular the lock gates, are new and will require a period of bedding in. Please take extra care when navigating to avoid damage.

NAVIGATION NOTES

HAWFORD

These notes are written as if travelling upstream on the Droitwich Canals from the River Severn to the Worcester & Birmingham Canal. Where specific notes refer to navigating in the opposite direction, they are shown with the legend '**DOWN**'.

The canal from Hawford to Droitwich is referred to as the Droitwich Barge Canal and has a nominal vessel width of 14ft (4.2 metres).

Hawford Junction seen from across the River Severn

Approaching the Droitwich Canal coming up the River Severn from Worcester, approximately half a mile after Bevere Lock the river bends to the left and you see a large cream house on the right bank. The Droitwich Barge Canal entrance lock is below this house. There is a pontoon below the lock on the left which is for lock use only (no mooring). There is also a pontoon on the right, against the river bank, which is a waiting area only, with no access to the bank or to the lock. No overnight mooring is allowed here.

If you are approaching downstream on the river, about three miles below Holt Lock, you approach a right hand bend. Do not mistake the entrance to the River Salwarpe for the canal entrance - there are no pontoons here. The canal entrance is marked by a large cream-painted house above the lock. If there is a current flowing, it is best to turn downstream of the lock on the bend, then come back up to the lock pontoons.

The River Salwarpe enters the Severn just upstream of the canal, and gives access to a boatyard.

The River Salwarpe accompanies the canal all the way to Droitwich.

DOWN: If going out onto river, take heed of the red, amber, green water level gauge outside the lock. The river current runs from right to left as you leave the canal.

Turning left towards Worcester, you are half a mile upstream of Bevere Lock. Ring when going downstream to request the lock keeper to get the lock ready for you. Telephone: 01905 640275. For opening hours of Bevere Lock, visit www.waterscape.com/canals-and-rivers/river-severn/boating/stoppages.

Turning right towards Stourport, you are 3 miles downstream of Holt Lock. Ring when going upstream. Telephone: 01905 620218

To travel upstream on the Severn, it is worth considering using the bankside pontoons, holding the fore end in and letting the current swing the stern round until the boat is facing upstream.

Hawford River Lock is now numbered as Lock No.1: previously it was thought that the locks on the Barge Canal were numbered from Droitwich, making this Lock 8. However, during dredging work associated with the restoration, a lock plate with the number 1 on it was found in the lock, confirming its former number. This is now affixed to the lock wall below the bottom gates.

HAWFORD

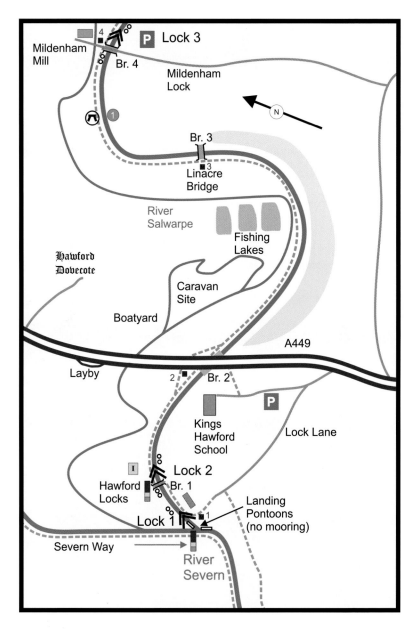

NOT TO SCALE   Approx 7 inches to 1 mile (10 cm = 1 km)

Note that the mooring bollards above this lock are on the offside (left)

Note that the locks on the Barge Canal do not have lower wing walls, so care is needed approaching the locks to steer accurately into them.

A short sweep of the canal brings you to Lock 2. The mooring bollards are again on the offside, (left) below the lock.

The towpath changes sides at Lock 2, proceeding on the left bank all the way to Droitwich.

The mooring bollards above the lock are on the right.

DOWN: Take heed of the red, amber, green water level gauge below Lock 2. This area is in the flood plain and despite being some distance from the river, it does flood.

Above Lock 2, on the offside beware of the protruding private canoe stage for use by the school. The school is a daughter school to Kings School Worcester, and its fields and buildings can be seen across the grounds above Lock 2. To the left can be glimpsed the fine arched stone bridge which carries the A449 road over the River Salwarpe.

The short tunnel (Bridge 2) under the dual carriageway A449 road has a cantilevered towpath throughout with handrails, although it is unlit.

Note the folding platforms on the offside wall before and after the bridge for use when installing stop planks.

The headroom reduces slightly at the upstream end of the tunnel.

There are mature woods above and to the right of the canal, which takes a pleasant long sweep, that brings you to Bridge 3 (Linacre Bridge), a fine old original red sandstone structure.

The views now open out on both sides to reveal distant hills and rolling fields. The approach to the next lock is heralded by mature trees on both sides of the canal.

At Lock 3 (Mildenham Lock), note that the mooring bollards above the lock are on the offside (right). There is a small public car park at Mildenham Lock.

The Pontoons at the entrance to Hawford Lock 1 on the River Severn

LADYWOOD

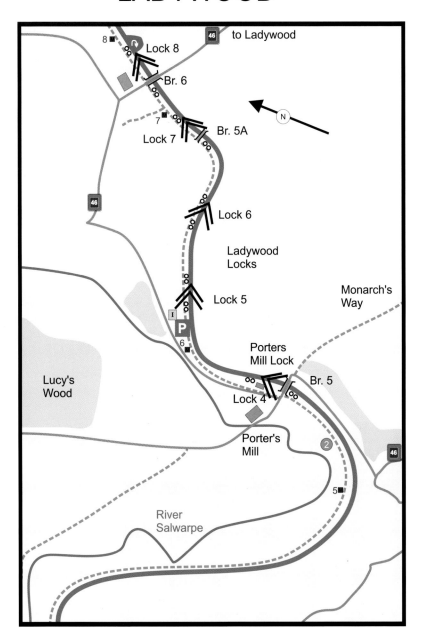

NOT TO SCALE   Approx 7 inches to 1 mile (10 cm = 1 km)

LADYWOOD

Above Mildenham Lock, the landscape opens out with rolling hills on both sides.

A long wooded stretch of canal brings you to Porter's Mill Lock (Lock 4). A road bridge (Bridge 5) crosses the canal below the lock. The lock cottage is now a private house.

To set the lock, a crew member must go up to the road bridge, cross the bridge to the other side of the canal and use the wooden gate next to the bridge to gain access to the lock. There is fencing between the cottage and the lock. On leaving the lock, crew will either have to get on board at the mooring bollards, or go out through the gates ahead., using a Watermate key.

DOWN: To set the lock when approaching on foot, go through the gate marked 'for lock use only' to reach the lock (a Watermate key is needed). On leaving the lock, after closing the bottom gates, crew must leave the lock by the gate next to the bridge, then cross the road bridge to regain the towpath.

Watch out for fishing on the stretch above this lock.

You are now in the Ladywood flight of five locks, spaced out over a half mile. As you rise in the flight, the countryside opens out to either side, as the canal leaves the valley of the River Salwarpe for a spell. Lock 6 has an unusual circular by-weir.

There is a footbridge over the tail of Lock 7 carrying a public footpath across the canal.

A modern road bridge crosses below Lock 8, with no towpath under it. You must cross the road to operate the lock.

Take care passing between the bridge abutments which are square and unprotected.

There are short cranked beams on the bottom gates of this lock because of the proximity of the road to the lock, where the original bridge was demolished when the road was widened. Look carefully to see the old abutments under the new concrete deck.

Lock 8 has a covered by-weir with a square inlet.

DOWN: Note that the top cills on the Barge Canal locks are semi-circular, so the greatest length is available in the centre of the lock.

SALWARPE

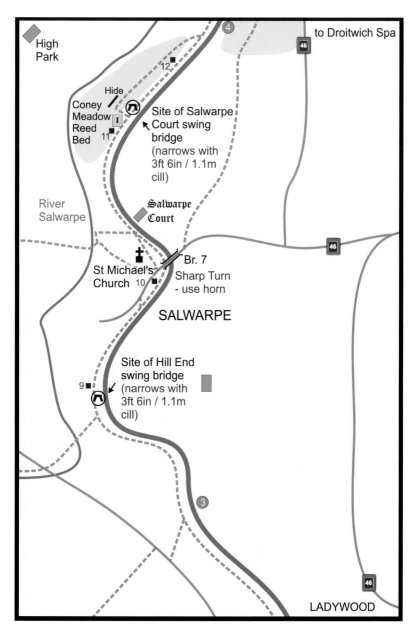

High Park

to Droitwich Spa

46

12

Hide

Coney
Meadow
Reed
Bed

I

11

Site of Salwarpe
Court swing
bridge
(narrows with
3ft 6in / 1.1m
cill)

River
Salwarpe

4

Salwarpe
Court

46

St Michael's
Church

10

Br. 7

Sharp Turn
- use horn

SALWARPE

Site of Hill End
swing bridge
(narrows with
3ft 6in / 1.1m
cill)

9

3

46

LADYWOOD

NOT TO SCALE   Approx 7 inches to 1 mile (10 cm = 1 km)

SALWARPE

The canal is tree-lined on the right, but to the left there are fine views across open countryside before the river approaches the canal again.

Hill End Swing Bridge is disused and not numbered, but the narrows remain, with a shallow cill at 3ft 6ins (1.1m) below normal water level. There is a picnic table next to the towpath by the narrows for this bridge.

Salwarpe church tower can be seen as you approach the village, and the reeds cease here for a stretch through the cutting. The village is heralded by a long brick wall on the right which protects a private road.

Approaching the tiny village of Salwarpe, there is access from the towpath to the village through a wooden gate. The canal now enters a deep cutting and Bridge 7 at Salwarpe is placed on a very sharp left hand bend in the canal - use the horn to warn any approaching boats.

In the arch of the bridge, a pair of insulators still attached to the bridge show that telegraph lines use to run alongside the canal here. The strange rows of square holes in the bridge arch were used to locate timber supports during the construction of the bridge.

As you pass through the cutting, a glimpse of the glorious half-timbered Salwarpe Court is visible high up on the right. The towpath is narrow under the bridge and through the cutting, and cyclists should dismount here.

At the eastern end of the cutting, there is a footpath from the towpath back to the churchyard of St Michael's and All Angels in Salwarpe.

There are also paths down through the woods over the River Salwarpe.

Emerging from the cutting, there are views to the left over the river valley and the Coney Meadow.

Salwarpe Court Swing Bridge is disused and not numbered, but the bridge narrows remain, with a shallow cill at 3ft 6 ins(1.1m) below normal water level..

There is a picnic table by the abandoned swing bridge. Also, this is the main entrance to the Coney Meadow Reed Bed.

Salwarpe Bridge

CHAWSON VALLEY

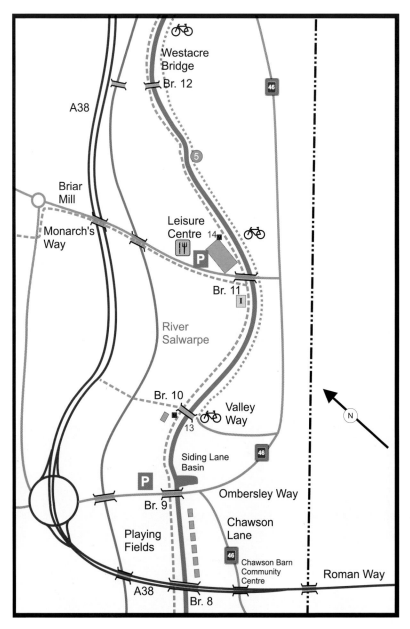

NOT TO SCALE   Approx 7 inches to 1 mile (10 cm = 1 km)

CHAWSON VALLEY

The sound of road traffic indicates where the A38 dual carriageway crosses on the Roman Way road bridge (Bridge No. 8). There is some parking in the layby at the top of the hill towards Worcester.

There is a path down to and along the river bank here.

The canal is now entering Droitwich, and although some houses are visible on the right, the canal is lined with mature hedges and the houses do not intrude. Houses are set back from the canal all the way into Droitwich on the right, but reeds continue on the towpath side. To the left are school and public playing fields and Droitwich Community Woods.

Immediately after Bridge 9, the Sidings Lane Basin can be seen on the right. It remains largely reed filled. Cyclists should take care between Bridges 8 and 9, due to the sandy nature of the towpath.

To the right hand side of the canal, there are still mature trees disguising the built up areas.

Just by Bridge 11, there is a Leisure Centre. Its grounds accompany the canal for some distance towards Bridge 12. There is a small canoe landing stage: do not use this as a mooring.

Bridge 10 on the Barge Canal

DROITWICH SPA

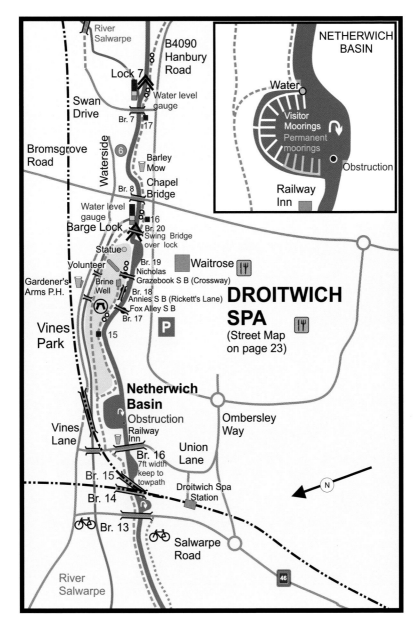

NOT TO SCALE   Approx 7 inches to 1 mile (10 cm = 1 km)

DROITWICH SPA

Approaching Bridge 13, the impressive railway signal box comes into view, set on an embankment. There is a sharp left turn just after Bridge 13.

At Bridge 13, the reeds on the towpath side cease, allowing access to the towpath.

Note that there is restricted navigation width under these bridges: only boats of 7ft 6 ins (2.1m) beam or less can proceed through Bridge 15. Broader beam boats should wind after Bridge 13. Keep to towpath side.

Bridge 14 carries the main railway line to Kidderminster, and is an impressive example of a brick-built skew bridge. As you approach there is time to marvel at the intricacy of its construction.

Passing under the second railway line to Bromsgrove at Bridge 15, there are various pieces of artwork in the tunnel, designed by local school children.

For railway buffs, this is one of last places you can still see the old Great Western semaphore signals in use.

The towpath leaves the canal after Bridge 15 - despite appearances, there is no way ahead under Bridge 16 to reach the basin. It is necessary to go up to the Kidderminster Road, cross the road and bear left to enter the park. Follow the footpath as it bears to the right to rejoin the canal at the basin.

Beside Bridge 16 is the Railway Inn.

The canal now enters Netherwich basin.

On the entrance to the basin, beware of the large concrete pedestal sticking up in the middle of the channel. This is thought to be a cap for the former brine well.

There are designated visitor moorings on the pontoons to the east side of the basin. A Watermate key is needed for access to and from the moorings. A water point is located on the finger to the canal side of the east pontoon. The basin forms one end of Vines Park, a pleasant open tree-lined grassy area.

DOWN: Before leaving Droitwich when travelling south, it is advisable to telephone British Waterways to establish whether the River Severn is in flood. Call the Gloucester Office on 01452 318000 or Bevere Lock on 01905 640275. For opening hours of Bevere Lock, visit www.waterscape.com/canals-and-rivers/river-severn/boating/stoppages.

DOWN: There is no towpath under Bridge 16: if following the canal from Vines Park, take the footpath through the park as it turns away from the canal basin, cross Kidderminster Road and rejoin the towpath before the railway bridge.

As the canal winds through the park, there are a series of three swing footbridges. The second of these will normally be fixed open to navigation. There are mooring bollards before the first one, and after the third. These bridges require a BW Watermate key to unlock them, and they then need to be swung open. They should be left closed or open, as you find them. The first bridge is pivoted on the offside, the second and third ones on the towpath side.

Beyond the final swing bridge, the canal widens on its approach to the next lock. The lock is offset to the left, and requires care on the approach to negotiate into position for the lock. There are no bollards on the approach to the lock.

All craft wider than 7ft (2.1m) should wind here. Although the lock is constructed to 'broad' dimensions, there is no suitable winding point past here.

This is Droitwich Barge Lock, and is the last of the broad beam locks. There is a swing footbridge over the middle of the lock, which must be unlocked and then swung open before the lock can be used. The bridge is pivoted on the off side (right).

Note the old quoins on the upstream end of the Lock, where a second set of gates enabled vessels to lock down as well as up into the River Salwarpe. Historically, due to brine pumping, the canal level was sometimes higher than that of the river.

Note: heed the red/amber/green flood warning signs at the exit from the Barge Lock.

DOWN: on approaching the Barge Lock from upstream, swing left to enter the lock, avoiding the river weir to the right.

DOWN: On leaving the Barge lock, it is necessary to push the front of the boat out from the wall to negotiate the sharp right angled turn at the exit of the lock.

Water from the Body Brook above enters the canal through a channel to the right of the Barge Lock, having been channelled down from above Lock 7 upstream. This helps to keep the River Salwarpe water separate while providing a water supply to the Barge Canal.

The section of canal from here to the foot of Lock 3 at Hanbury Wharf is a new construction, as the original line has been compromised in various places.

The canal upstream of the Barge Lock is suitable for narrow beam boats only, and is part of the later Junction Canal. Initially, it follows the course of the River Salwarpe under the road bridge and swings left. Ahead can be seen the opening through which the canal originally emerged. The river has been canalised and deepened as part of the canal restoration. After passing under the road bridge at Swan Drive, you head to the right to enter lock 7.

Note that Lock 7 is a newly-constructed lock and has no wing walls - so great care needs to be taken to enter it accurately between the bluff concrete walls.

Above Lock 7, a grating in the towpath indicates the by-wash that enables water to flow 500m underground to emerge below the Barge lock. This is to minimise the mixing of canal and river water.

Above Lock 7, the canal swings away from the road and we lose the towpath temporarily. To follow the towpath, join the road and walk across Impney Way, and under the M5 motorway.

DOWN: heed the red/amber/green flood warning signs at the exit of Lock 7.

Moorings in Netherwich Basin

JUNCTION CANAL

The canal above Lock 7 now widens and swings to the left, passing an overflow weir on the left.

On the left, you will see a waiting staging, where you can wait if boats are coming the other way through the M5 culvert. (On the right is a private mooring).

Proceed slowly to the next bridge (Impney Way): from here you can see ahead to the culvert under the M5 motorway. Since this culvert is not wide enough to permit boats to pass one another, do not proceed beyond here if you see a boat approaching through the culvert. It may be best to reverse to the waiting area for them to pass.

DOWN: To walk from Impney Way, follow the B4090 to rejoin the towpath above Lock 7.

Proceed with caution to the M5 culvert, and note the low headroom through the culvert (6ft 5ins/1.97m). You emerge passing under a metal footbridge which carries the towpath back over the canal.

If walking the B4090 cross Impney Way. At the mini roundabout after the M5, a side road to leads to Hadzor village. Instead, turn left and cross a metal footbridge to rejoin the canal bank.

DOWN: Above the M5 culvert, there is a waiting area on the offside. Stop here and look through the culvert to ensure that no boats are coming up, as the culvert is narrow.

Below Lock 6, the Body Brook enters the canal under the towpath.

DOWN: heed the red/amber/green flood warning signs at the exit of Lock 6

Above Lock 6, the pound widens. The water here is likely to be eddying if the staircase locks above have been in use recently.

Before using the staircase locks (when ascending) first make sure no boats are coming down. Then ensure the bottom lock of the staircase is empty and the top lock is full. Enter the bottom lock with great care, as there are no wing walls to guide the boat into the lock.

DOWN: Before using the staircase locks (when descending) first make sure no boats are coming up. Then ensure the bottom lock of the staircase is empty and the top lock is full. Enter the top lock with great care, as there are no wing walls to guide the boat into the lock.

The landing stage on the right above the staircase locks is private.

You now pass the Hanbury Gateway Park on your right before passing under the new bridge carrying the access road to Droitwich Rugby Football Club.

The towpath changes sides at the Rugby Club bridge.

By the bridge is a solar- powered water level monitor.

On the left is the entrance to the 238 berth Droitwich Spa Marina, due to open in autumn 2011.

You now regain the original line of the canal with the three Hanbury Locks ahead.

The existing line of the canal below Lock 3 has been left as a wildlife area.

Locks 1-3 are quite deep, so paddles should be opened slowly when ascending.

JUNCTION CANAL

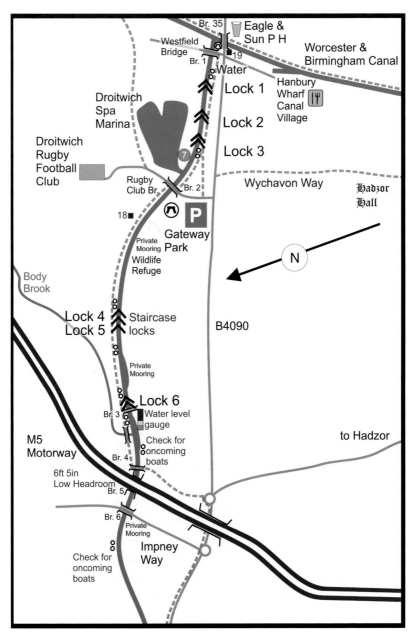

Br. 35

Eagle & Sun P H

Westfield Bridge

Br. 1

Worcester & Birmingham Canal

19

Water

Lock 1

Hanbury Wharf Canal Village

Droitwich Spa Marina

Lock 2

Lock 3

Droitwich Rugby Football Club

7

Rugby Club Br.

Br. 2

Wychavon Way

Hadzor Hall

18

P

Gateway Park

Private Mooring

Wildlife Refuge

Body Brook

Lock 4
Lock 5

Staircase locks

B4090

N

Private Mooring

Lock 6

Br. 3

Water level gauge

Check for oncoming boats

M5 Motorway

Br. 4

to Hadzor

6ft 5in Low Headroom

Br. 5

Br. 6

Private Mooring

Impney Way

Check for oncoming boats

NOT TO SCALE   Approx 7 inches to 1 mile (10 cm = 1 km)

These locks have side ponds, which were originally used to save water when using the locks - but these won't normally be in use.

There is a water point on the towpath above Lock 1.

Westfield Bridge by the junction carries a private road to the farm.

There is a small picnic area at the junction in memory of Brenda Morris, a former chair of the Worcester & Birmingham Canal Society.

Bridge 35 on the Worcester & Birmingham Canal is immediately on the right as you leave the Junction Canal. This is a tight turn out if going right towards Worcester, and the bridge makes it a blind exit, so give a long blast on the horn to warn other boaters, who will not yet be used to the idea of boats coming out of the Junction Canal.

On the main road, the Eagle & Sun pub offers food as well as liquid refreshment.

Hanbury Wharf Canal Village is just south of Bridge 35 and is the home of the New & Used Boat Co. There are also businesses offering chandlery, a cafe, diesel coal and gas, a marine engineer. a gift shop, and various local traders.

ENTERING THE DROITWICH JUNCTION CANAL FROM THE WORCESTER & BIRMINGHAM CANAL.
If coming from Worcester, the entry is a very tight left turn immediately after Bridge 35, straight into another narrow bridgehole. If approaching from the Tardebigge direction, the canal swings left and the entrance bridge is visible on the right.

Hanbury Junction where the Junction Canal meets the Worcester & Birmingham Canal

THE MID WORCESTERSHIRE RING

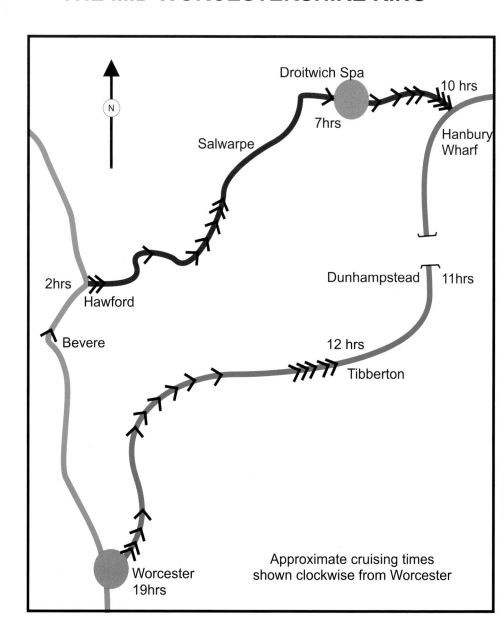

Droitwich Spa

10 hrs

7hrs

Hanbury Wharf

Salwarpe

N

Dunhampstead   11hrs

2hrs

Hawford

Bevere

12 hrs

Tibberton

Worcester
19hrs

Approximate cruising times
shown clockwise from Worcester

THE MID-WORCESTERSHIRE RING

This 21-mile cruising loop was made possible by the re-opening of the Droitwich Canals. The ring can also form a distance walk, using part of the Severn Way, then the towpaths of the Droitwich and Worcester & Birmingham canals.

Starting in the cathedral city of Worcester, the route is first down two deep locks at Diglis onto the River Severn (having checked that water levels on the river are suitable for safe navigation). Heading upstream, the river passes almost underneath the imposing cathedral and then the fine stone five-arched bridge. This is followed by the main line railway on a high iron viaduct and then the famous racecourse, where there are moorings. The river winds through pleasant wooded countryside to Bevere Lock (pronounced Bevery), four miles from Worcester. The Camp House Inn is situated just south of the lock here. For opening hours of Bevere Lock, visit www.waterscape.com/canals-and-rivers/river-severn/boating/stoppages.

A mile beyond Bevere, the river swings right and as it swings back, you will see the entrance lock to the Droitwich Barge Canal on the right. There are pontoons on the left of the lock entrance to wait while you prepare the lock.

Navigation of the Droitwich Canals is covered elsewhere in this book, so we pick up the ring again by turning right out of the Droitwich Junction Canal onto the Worcester & Birmingham Canal at Hanbury Wharf.

In two miles, after passing within the impressive sight of Hadzor Hall on the right, you reach the north portal of the short Dunhampstead tunnel (which has no towpath - the path diverts over the top of the hill). Beyond the tunnel is a boatyard (Brook Line Narrowboats) and moorings for The Fir Tree pub, before you enter a wooded cutting.

In a further two miles, at Tibberton village, there are also moorings. The village has two pubs, the Bridge Inn and Speed the Plough and a village shop and post office selling basic provisions and newspapers. After Tibberton, the canal passes under the M5 motorway and descends the five Offerton Locks. Tolladine Lock marks the beginning of the entry into Worcester, and there are six locks quite close together here. After a short space, a fine railway viaduct appears spanning the canal, and this is followed by a boatyard on the right (Viking Afloat). Above Sidbury Lock there are moorings for the Civil War Commandery Museum. Below this, you enter Diglis Basin which has more moorings and precedes the locks down to the river Severn.

The Barge Lock in Vines Park

SERVICES ON THE DROITWICH CANALS

Most services are available in Droitwich Spa, including:

TOURISM
Tourist Information Centre, Victoria Square 01905 774312

MEDICAL
Doctors:
Droitwich Medical Centre, Ombersley Street East 01905 681000
36 Corbett Avenue.. 01905 795566

DENTISTS:
67 Ombersley Street East 01905 778873
83 Friar Street... 01905 799228
2 Old Market Court, High Street 01905 797733
47 Blackfriars Avenue.. 01905 779956

PHARMACIES:
Droitwich Pharmacy, 53 Ombersley Street East
St Mary's Pharmacy, Farmers Way
Droitwich Medical Centre, Ombersley Street East
Boots, 50 St Andrews Square

VETS:
North Street.. 01905 772002
36 Hanbury Road 01905 773262

PUBS & RESTAURANTS:
Barley Mow, 9 Hanbury Street, Droitwich, Worcestershire WR9 8PL 01905 773248
Eagle & Sun, Hanbury Junction, Droitwich 01905 770130
The Hop Pole, 40 Friar Street, Droitwich 01905 770155
The Old Cock Inn, 77 Friar Street, Droitwich 01905 774233
Railway Inn, Kidderminster Road, Droitwich (by Netherwich basin) 01905 770056
Gardeners Arms, Vines Lane (by Vines Park).. 01905 772936
Rossini Restaurant, 6 Worcester Road, Droitwich 01905 794799

PUBLIC TRANSPORT
Trains run to Droitwich from Birmingham via Kidderminster or
Bromsgrove and from Worcester. 08457 484950
Buses run to Droitwich from Bromsgrove, Hanbury, Kidderminster,
Redditch and Worcester 0871 200 2233

BRITISH WATERWAYS
Gloucester Area Office 01452 318000
Emergency number.. 0800 4799947
Bevere Lock... 01905 640275

Up to date information about the Droitwich Canals is available at www.waterscape.com/droitwich

ACCOMMODATION
Contact the Tourist Information Centres in Droitwich Spa (01905 774312) or Worcester (01905 726311), or visit the county tourist web site at www.visitworcestershire.org

BOAT YARDS
Hanbury Canal Village on the Worcester & Birmingham Canal at Hanbury Wharf 01905 771018
Moorings, slipway, water, refuse, elsan, fuel, gas, repairs, chandlery

DROITWICH SPA MARINA
at the foot of Lock 3 on the Junction Canal. ....07837 072463 www.droitwichspamarina.co.uk
Moorings, pump out, fuel , laundry

GEORGE JUDGE
on the River Salwarpe at Hawford 01905 458705
Gas, repairs, chandlery

WATER POINT
Netherwich Basin, Droitwich
Hanbury Wharf

HIRE BOATS
Viking Afloat, Lowesmoor Wharf, Worcester ....08451 264098 www.viking-afloat.com
Brook Line Narrowboats, Dunhampstead Wharf ....01905 773889 www.brookline.co.uk
Black Prince Holidays, Stoke Prior ....01527 575115 www.black-prince.com
Starline Narrowboats, Upton on Severn Marina ....01531 632003 www.starlinenarrowboats.co.uk
UK Boat Hire, Alvechurch..0330 3330 560 www.ukboathire.com
Portharb, Northwick Marina, Worcester..01905 29938 www.portharb.com
Anglo Welsh Waterway Holidays, Tardebigge ....0117 304 1122 www.anglowelsh.co.uk

SERVICES ELSEWHERE ON THE MID WORCESTERSHIRE RING

RIVER SEVERN
PUB
Camp House, Camp Lane, Grimley (below Bevere lock) 01905 640288

Mooring and water point at Worcester Racecourse
Water point and Elsan above Diglis Lock

WORCESTER & BIRMINGHAM CANAL
PUBS:
The Fir Tree, Dunhampstead (by Bridge 30)..01905 774094
Bridge Inn, Plough Road, Tibberton (by Bridge 25)..01905 345874
Speed the Plough, Plough Road, Tibberton (by Bridge 25) 01905 345602
Cavalier, 107 St Georges Lane North, Worcester (below Lock 5)....................................01905 25006
Anchor, 54 Diglis Road, Worcester (by Diglis Basin) 01905 351094

BOAT YARD
Viking Afloat, Lowesmoor Wharf, Worcester (by Bridge 9) 01905 612707
Mooring, water, elsan, pumpout, gas, diesel

Water point and Elsan in Diglis Basin

THE NATURAL YEAR ON THE CANAL

by Geoff Trevis (Chairman, Droitwich Spa Local Group, Worcestershire Wildlife Trust)

The first of January - the depth of winter. It may be cold and bright with frost or snow but more likely it is going to be cold and wet with dripping vegetation and little sign of life. But one year I went out for a walk on New Year's Day, following the canal from Ombersley Way to Ladywood. It was remarkably mild with a winter sun just setting in the afternoon and a bat was hawking over the water near Salwarpe, feeding on the winter gnats that had emerged into the sunlight. Whatever the time of year, you can never know what will be about! Sometimes the trees and bushes seem full of birds, whilst damselflies and dragonflies patrol the water and reed beds and butterflies, bees and other insects fill the air with colour and a gentle hum. All this animal life is supported by the many plants which grow in season in, by and near the canal. At other times one can walk the tow path and see little worth noting. One never knows and that is part of the pleasure - what will I find today?

The canal corridor provides one of the few areas where wildlife has thrived undisturbed for many years. Species from woodland, grassland, water and reed bed appear in close proximity and the development of Coney Meadow has added to the diversity. A short walk off the towpath at Coney Meadow can provide sight of wading birds, ducks on ponds and lakes, and dragonflies more often associated with still water. Canal restoration did affect some species, especially dragonflies and damselflies but only temporarily. Variety is a feature of the Droitwich Canals which encompass water, reed beds and grassland within the canal corridor, and are surrounded by urban areas, farmland, grazed fields, woodland, old orchards and gardens. They play host to a wide variety of creatures. Nonetheless, we must be aware that much diversity arises from the surrounding land and its management will profoundly affect what we will see as we walk the towpath or observe the wildlife from a boat.

What you will see on any walk depends not only on the season but how far advanced or retarded it is. In some years spring will be evident in the flowers in early February whilst in other years little can be found until well into March. In the following discussion, therefore, months are treated with some caution and the changes are related to seasons.

WINTER

Winter is the quietest time for wildlife whether along the canal or in the wider countryside. There are few, if any, flowers or insects and it is a time for looking up rather than down. The winter skies can be quite spectacular and the low sunlight brings out all the texture and subdued colour of the landscape. Birds provide the main interest and the list of resident species along the canal is long. It includes black-headed and lesser black-backed gulls, wood pigeons, collared doves, greater spotted and green woodpeckers, pied wagtails, starlings, carrion crows, rooks, jackdaws, magpies, jays, wrens, robins, dunnocks, blackcaps, blackbirds, song thrushes, mistle thrushes, house sparrows, chaffinches, greenfinches, bullfinches, reed buntings, yellowhammers, mallard, coots, moorhens, little grebes (or dabchicks), swans, buzzards, kestrels, sparrow hawks and herons. In winter, tits congregate into parties which forage in the hedges. Blue tits, great tits, long-tailed tits and coal tits may be seen together. Kingfishers may generally be seen all through the year, but in very harsh weather when the water is frozen they migrate to the coasts where the higher temperatures provide more equitable conditions for feeding. It is always worth keeping an eye on the skies above where cormorants, lapwings and the occasional raven can be seen.

The number of species will be increased in winter by the migrants or species moving into the area to find food and shelter. Most obvious among the migrants are the two thrushes, redwings and fieldfares but in some seasons more unusual birds can seen, for example waxwings or bramblings. The thrushes may be seen in large mixed flocks, up to several hundred strong, or in small groups feeding in the fields or on the hedgerow berries whilst waxwings are particularly attracted to rowan, and bramblings are usually in the company of chaffinches. Teal, curlew, snipe and other waders have been recorded in Coney Meadow.

Winter is also the time for seeing the signs of mammal activity. The presence of mammals may be evident in tracks in snow; through identifying gnawed hazel nuts or other fruit; occasionally through droppings such those left by otters or mink or in badger latrines; and through regularly used paths in canal side vegetation. Apart from rabbits, the only mammal you are likely to see is the fox which will be out hunting during the few hours of daylight. Flowers will be few and far between and the only insects you may encounter will be the winter gnats, a few hoverflies on warm days and the occasional butterfly tempted out of hibernation when the temperature rises.

But nature never sleeps. Even in January you will see the hazel catkins expanding to shed their pollen and woodland plants such as dog's mercury may start to flower in very mild seasons. In February things will usually start to grow, unless we have a very prolonged, severe winter, and the yellow stars of lesser celandine have been noted as early as mid-February.

Swans on the Barge Canal above Porters Mill Lock

SPRING

The transition from winter to spring is probably the most exciting time of year. Gradually the browns and soft greens and yellows provided by lichens give way to the fresh greens of growing plants and quite soon the first flowers will appear. Spring is generally the time of woodland plants which need to flower before the trees come in to leaf and cut off the life-giving sunshine. First come the snowdrops, so prolific in the cutting at Salwarpe, closely followed by coltsfoot and primroses. Violets, forget-me-nots, speedwells, bluebells and cowslips will soon be on the scene as the cow parsley, hogweed and hemlock start to grow prior to flowering. The vast array of plants is too numerous for a complete list to be included here and a little time spent on the towpath with a suitable handbook will amply repay the effort. Of course, there are the many plants which seem to continue flowering throughout the year such as dandelion, daisy, red and white dead nettles, hawkweeds etc. all of which are vital to insects in providing nectar and pollen. In return the insects carry out the process of pollination, except for the dandelions which are self-pollinating. Slightly later in spring red and white campion flower, as do the buttercups, wild arum (also known as cuckoo pint), herb robert, herb bennett (or wood avens) and cuckoo flower (lady's smock).

Spring is also the time when the first insects will be seen. Usually red admiral, brimstone, comma and peacock butterflies will be the first to appear as they are tempted out of hibernation by the warm sunshine and orange tips and holly blues will soon follow. These will be closely followed by queen bumblebees, also emerging from winter's hibernation and looking to feed before finding nest sites to establish new colonies of workers. Close attention to vegetation will yield additional records of various ladybirds and shield bugs whilst hoverflies and solitary bees emerge to begin  their annual cycle. The early dandelions and the pussy willows are vital as food sources for these insects and it is well worth spending time looking at pussy willow, especially if you have binoculars with you. Also vital to the early insects are the flowers of blackthorn which bring the hedges to life.

Spring is the time of the great changeover for the migrant birds. Redwings and fieldfares will leave for their breeding grounds to be replaced by the many species returning from warmer climates. Undoubtedly the first migrant will be the chiff-chaff, making its presence known through its monotonous call - so welcome in early March but quickly becoming something of an irritant as the season progresses. March is also likely to witness the return of sand martins, which do not breed near the canal but which can be seen flying about collecting insects, on their way to the sandy banks where they will establish their nest tunnels. In April the swallows and house martins will arrive along with willow warblers, whitethroats, reed and sedge warblers and the occasional grasshopper warbler. May will see the arrival of the last migrants, the cuckoos and swifts. One interesting species is the grey wagtail which, though resident in Britain, is rarely seen along the canal corridor in winter but is regularly recorded through the spring and summer. These species will be resident in the area but a watch on the hedges and skies may yield records of other species in passage such as stonechats, whinchats, redstarts or hobbies. On one occasion a male hen harrier was seen flying close to the canal. Not every possible species is listed so always keep an eye open for the more unexpected and unusual ones.

At the end of April the trees will be coming into leaf and the leaf covered hawthorns will be coming into flower. This is a vital time for many birds. The young foliage provides the food source for a myriad of insect larvae, pre-eminent among which are the larvae of oak tortrix and winter moths which can strip an oak tree almost bare. These larvae are the main food collected by birds to feed their growing young and several hundred may be needed each day. If egg laying and hatching is not synchronised with the emergence of the larvae there is a disaster as young birds may well starve to death in the nest. If all is well disaster is averted and the trees benefit by having the caterpillar population reduced to an acceptable level. When oaks are stripped almost bare they often produce a second flush of leaves of a reddish colour known as lammas growth. By summer the leaves will have become tough and infused with tannin making them generally unattractive to insects.

Of course, a major feature of the canal is water. During the winter and spring, as noted above, the only item of interest associated with this habitat is the birdlife. However, by late spring much else will be coming to life. The earliest damselfly to emerge is likely to be the large red damselfly followed by the banded and beautiful demoiselles and the blue banded common and azure damselflies. The male demoiselles are spectacular with their metallic blue bodies. The male banded demoiselle has, as its name suggests, dark bands on the wings whilst the beautiful female demoiselle has more diffuse darker wing patches. At the same time as the damselflies are emerging you will see the first water boatmen and whirligig beetles in sheltered water among the reeds, especially near the fishing stations and shoals of red-finned roach will patrol near the water surface.

Soils in the area are fairly alkaline with available calcium. This is ideal for snails which need the calcium to build their shells. In warm, damp weather the banded snails climb the taller vegetation and can be easily observed. Some people may wonder why on earth one would wish to observe snails but actually they are a diverse and interesting group. Just look at the banded snails whose colours vary from a light greenish yellow, without bands, to specimens with broad, dark brown bands and virtually no light colour at all. These snails have been used as experimental animals by geneticists in tracking the genes responsible for colour variation. There is also a snail which is pinkish brown in colour with a darker colour close to the edge of the shell where the snail emerges. This is the Kentish snail which is usually found in limestone areas. There are of course the common garden snails and also a host of very small snails which have yet to be studied in the vicinity of the canal. All these snails will start to appear as the weather warms in spring.

SUMMER

Summer is the time of long and, hopefully for some of the time, hot sunny days. After the exuberance of spring it is a time of consolidation for wildlife as families are raised and, later in the season, a time for feeding up in preparation for the coming winter. Some birds will have finished breeding whilst others will be raising second or even third broods. There will be little change in species from those seen in the late spring. Ducks and swans will be out on the water with their flotillas of young, and adults of some other species will be seen still feeding young in the fields or hedges. A notable feature of bird life-style is the silence, particularly in August. This is the time, having generally raised their broods, that they undertake the annual moult and thus do not want to advertise their presence to potential predators. Sometimes you will see August referred to as the silent month. Only later will bird song increase again as they start to re-establish territories. August is also the month that some summer migrants begin their return to their winter quarters. The swift is among the first to go.

Early summer is the time to look for meadow flowers which bloom much later than their woodland cousins. The umbellifers, cow parsley, hogweed and hemlock will be in full flower attracting a wide range of bees, wasps, flies and beetles. The brownish-red soldier beetles will be seen on nearly all the flowers but they seem to have a particular liking for hogweed. In many places along the canal the taller vegetation is dominated by hemlock. This is a most attractive plant with finely cut leaves, red blotches on the stem and reaching a height up to about eight feet. The record is one about 14 feet high which was growing under trees and hence putting on height to reach the light. As summer progresses the cow parsley goes to seed and its place is taken by similar looking umbellifers, upright hedge-parsley and rough chervil. Up to thirty three species of plant have been recorded in flower at one time in June so a full list would make tedious reading. However, the most prominent include (in no particular order) meadow, creeping and bulbous buttercups, marsh and hedge woundwort, wild carrot, forget-me-not, iris, ground ivy, dog and field roses, common and tufted vetch, water figwort, creeping, spear and welted thistles, self heal, black medick, bitter-sweet, white bryony, hawkweeds and hedge bedstraw. Later in the summer great and rosebay willow herbs provide displays of purple along with black knapweed, and sow thistles, fleabane, lady's bedstraw and hawkbits add bright splashes of yellow. It  is also at this time that the common toadflax will be seen and this seems to signal the approaching end of summer and the onset of autumn. Wild clematis has become established in several places. Its flowers are less than striking, being rather small and pale cream, but its fluffy seed heads stand out giving the plant its common name of old man's beard. Two plants deserve special attention for different reasons. In Coney Meadow and in several places along the edge of the canal there are strong growths of celery leaved buttercup. This is not generally common and one can only suppose that it has been introduced in wetland seed mixtures. The other species for special mention is the beautiful but ecologically disastrous himalayan balsam. The purple flowers brighten many a wet bank or moist bit of woodland but it is able to spread rapidly through seed and small pieces of stem. It has few, if any, natural predators and can become dominant to the extent that it will suppress and eventually eradicate the native flora. A constant war against it is needed to keep it in bounds.

Insects, of course, abound in summer and it is a case of where to start describing them. Most people will notice the butterflies and dragonflies and both will be seen on the towpath or from a boat. Often

June can be poor for butterflies as the larvae of spring species have not yet emerged as adults and the summer species have yet to appear. However, in late June and July and through into August many species can be ticked off the list which will include (in no particular order) small, green-veined and large whites, small tortoiseshell, peacock, painted lady, comma, red admiral, small skipper, large skipper, essex skipper, speckled wood, marbled white, common blue, holly blue, brown argus, small copper, meadow brown, gate keeper and ringlet. A few day flying moths might also be seen, especially the spectacular red and black cinnabar moths and burnets or a humming bird hawk moth hovering in front of a flower.

The larger dragonflies will be putting in an appearance along with their smaller damselfly cousins. By summer the demoiselles will have completed their season but some of the small blue damselflies can still be found. The air will now be the territory of brown hawkers, common hawkers, southern hawkers, four-spotted and broad-bodied chasers, black-tailed skimmers, Emperors and common and ruddy darters. Towards the end of the summer the migrant hawker seems more common and is one of the species that seems to say 'autumn is on the way'. There are several species of dragonflies that are expanding their range in Britain or starting to visit or even breed here for the first time so it is well worth checking up on what you see. You may get a first county record.

Most other insect groups will be reaching peak abundance over the summer months and looking closely at flowers and leaves can be very rewarding. The bees, wasps and hoverflies will stand out but, unfortunately, many of them can only be identified by an expert with a microscope. Nonetheless, social wasps and bumblebees can easily be seen and the bumblebees often identified to species. There are six common bumblebee species - Buff-tailed, white-tailed, red-tailed, common carder, small-garden and early - which will be illustrated in many insect books. With a bit more care you may also be able to recognise one of the cuckoo bees whose English name is the vestal cuckoo-bee and the relatively newly arrived tree bumblebee (Bombus hypnorum). Later in the season, if you look at ivy blossom, you will see a huge range of bees, wasps, hoverflies, beetles and other insects and occasionally you will be rewarded by a glimpse of a very large queen hornet. Ladybird spotting is also a fun pastime. Of course, the ubiquitous seven spot ladybird will be easily found but a bit of hunting will find the red and black two spot, ten-spot and twenty four spot species and the black and yellow fourteen-spot, sixteen-spot and 22-spot species. Occasionally the water ladybird has also been recorded. Inspection of the reed leaves often brings to light the newest of our ladybirds, the harlequin. This is a very variable species which has been extending its range across the country and has caused some concern because it attacks and eats the larvae of other ladybirds and thereby may seriously reduce the numbers of the native species. Only time will tell whether this concern is justified. It is worth looking carefully when harlequins are found as often the larvae, pupae newly emerged adults and older adults can be seen together. Newly emerged ladybirds of most species are yellow with indistinct or pale markings which can cause confusion until they gradually develop their usual adult colours.

An interesting side line of entomology and botany is that of the plant galls. These are the abnormal growths on plants and trees caused by insects which lay their eggs in the plant tissue. When the larvae emerge they feed in the gall safely protected from many predators. But they do not have it all their own way. There are flies and wasps which lay eggs in the developing gall whose larvae benefit from the nutritious gall tissue and there are parasites which lay eggs in or close to the larvae of the gall former or the intruders whose larvae are carnivorous and in turn make a meal of the vegetarian larvae already present. Along the canal you can find the many oak galls. There are the wrinkled galls on the acorn cups, the knopper galls, there are smooth, round marble galls, oak apple galls and artichoke galls and small, round, flat, brown silk button and oyster galls on the leaves. And if you look at some of the rather weak, spindly roses growing close to the water on the edge of the canal you may find red, hairy looking galls called bedeguar or robins pin cushion galls. The galls are caused by small wasps, flies and mites.

AUTUMN

Like spring, this is a time of change and also a time of spectacular beauty as the trees put on their autumn colours before leaf fall. Early in the season many of the species of late summer will be about including butterflies, dragonflies, bees, wasps and hoverflies. Most flowers and trees will have developed seeds and fruits, all of which add to the character of the season. Hedges will contain red berries on the hawthorn, guelder rose and bitter-sweet along with red rose hips and black blackberries, sloes and elderberries whilst seeds of reeds and willow herbs will drift on the breeze.

Fungi are a special feature of early autumn, usually appearing in September and October until the frosts kill them off. The canal towpath and adjoining fields are unfortunately rather lacking in this fascinating group but you will often find the large caps of the parasol mushroom, and lawyer's wig or shaggy ink caps sprouting from the grass. The other species are generally small brown grassland species or groups of white or brown toadstools on rotting logs. Other than this the bracket fungi on trees are the most likely to be seen. With regular mowing along the towpath we may eventually get the colourful waxcaps but none of these has yet been recorded.

Often there will be a good range of insects to be seen until frost intervenes. Southern hawker and common red darter dragonflies are the most frequent of this group though migrant hawkers and others may still be encountered. The ivy blossom, as in late summer, remains perhaps the most important source of nectar and as such it will attract the last butterflies, bees, hoverflies etc. Late season butterflies include red admiral, comma, small tortoiseshell, speckled wood and 'whites'. In the nests of social wasps and bumblebees the social structure of the colony will be breaking down and the remaining workers and males will continue feeding themselves whilst the queens go into hibernation. The latest bumblebee to be seen is likely to be the brown common carder bee as this seems to have a longer season than many other species except perhaps the buff-tailed bumblebee.

As summer ends we lose the warblers, swallows and martins but prepare to welcome the fieldfares and redwings and the passage migrants moving south before winter arrives. It is always worth looking for those other rarer winter species – the waxwing and the brambling - and Coney Meadow will merit a visit if the water level is high enough to provide mud as snipe and other waders may be there. Otherwise it will be the usual British residents which will be coming into view in the binoculars.

If the weather is mild the wildlife interest will continue into November but usually this is the month when nature shuts down. By the end of the month little will be seen from boat or from the towpath. A few last flowers may hang on the yarrow but there are not sufficient to maintain the insect population so the only entomological interest will be the winter 'gnats' dancing in the patches of sunshine on mild days and the occasional red admiral or small tortoiseshell roused from hibernation. But, as previously noted, nature never sleeps. Birds and mammals continue their activity and don't forget those hazel trees whose catkins will soon extend and ripen ready to shed pollen and begin another year.

THE DROITWICH GREEN NECKLACE

by Roger Claxton (Tree Warden, Droitwich Woods)

The Droitwich Green Necklace pathway follows a continuous circular route of approximately 7 miles around the outskirts of Droitwich Spa. Walkers can access it in many places from the housing areas and, using a section of it, can access country paths forming circular walks. The Green Necklace is a major pedestrian in-feed to the canal corridor, adjacent to the Droitwich ring road bridge. It connects the large housing area of The Ridings (and the projected Copcut housing area) to the canal via Droitwich community woods. The Green Necklace then becomes the canal towpath all the way to Droitwich and along the Junction Canal, leaving the path where it is crossed by the M5. Along this Salwarpe valley section where Droitwich community woods abut the canal there are several circular way-marked walks that canal users can access to enjoy playing fields, woodland, grassland, marsh and wetland habitats. This area was a SSSI site as (due to the saline conditions), many plants normally found at the coast flourish eg wild carrot and dittander. In fact, hidden under the grass on the bank that sweeps down to the stream in the Gorsey Bank section of the reserve is an inland sand dune. This was formed on the shores of a sea millions of years ago when our land mass was south of the equator - a sea that produced the salt deposits that put the 'wich' into Droitwich.

The Green Necklace is a Droitwich Spa Civic Society initiative, supported by county and district councils. Droitwich Community Woods are owned by Wychavon District Council and managed by Worcestershire Wildlife Trust.

The Barge Canal at Westacre

DROITWICH CANAL WALKS

by Mick Yarker

These nine walks between them cover almost the whole length of the Droitwich Canals, as well as giving a taste of the surrounding countryside. The start points of the walks are shown on the map on page 9. They are not particularly long walks, but some may be over paths not often frequented. In general, the paths are marked by way-marks that usually consist of a yellow arrow on a white disc affixed to a post or fence. These are often visible right across a field when you get used to looking for them.

Some parts of the walks may be muddy at any time of year, so stout footwear is recommended. I also recommend obtaining the Ordnance Survey Explorer 204 map to take on these walks. It shows the whole of the Droitwich Canals and the Mid Worcestershire Ring.

All these walks begin with a short drive from Droitwich, which is used as a reference starting point. The walks are arranged in geographical order, starting at the River Severn.

If you fancy a longer walk, you can find a description of the walk from Droitwich to Worcester via the Barge Canal and the River Severn at www.waterscape.com/droitwich.

The Barge Lock seen from upstream, with the River Salwarpe on the right

Walk No. 1. Bevere   Distance: 3 miles

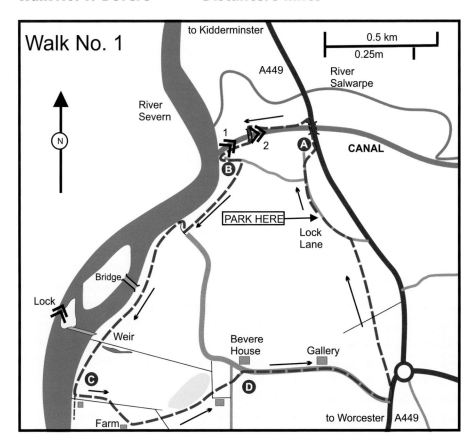

Walk No. 1

to Kidderminster

0.5 km
0.25m

A449

River
Salwarpe

River
Severn

CANAL

N

1
2

A

B

PARK HERE

Lock
Lane

Bridge

Lock

Weir

Bevere
House

Gallery

C

D

Farm

to Worcester   A449

This walk takes in the lower end of the Barge Canal and a section of the Severn which forms part of the Mid Worcestershire Ring. The walk takes about an hour and a half. The section near the Severn may be impassable in times of flood, so please bear this in mind. Please keep dogs on a lead. The walk features several stiles and some muddy bits, so mini skirts and stilettos are not recommended.

To get there from Droitwich, drive south down the A38 towards Worcester, turn off right just beyond the big road bridge after Fernhill Heath (sign-posted to Claines). Go straight on at Claines, then take the second exit off the Northern Link roundabout and head towards Kidderminster on the A449. After a few hundred yards turn off left down Lock Lane (clearly sign-posted) and park on the lane as soon as you find a safe spot.

Leaving the car, walk straight ahead down the lane, continuing on at the 'no entry' road sign by Hawford School. At the dead end of this old section of road a path rises on the right to the new A449 alignment on a higher level and further to the east. You are now at **Point A.**

Turn left and walk along the A449 pavement northwards over the new tunnel. This passes under the dual carriageway on the skew and hence is long enough to be considered a tunnel. In Brindley's day the canal had a pronounced dogleg here so that it could pass under the then narrow road at 90 degrees with a conventional arched brick bridge.

Immediately after passing over the tunnel, turn left down a path into a field. Go through the gate and continue straight ahead along the towpath with the canal to your left. If you look behind you to the right, you will see the massive road bridge over the River Salwarpe. Follow the towpath to the lock (Lock 2) about 200 yards further ahead. Cross the bridge here and walk along the new footpath to the right. The Trust workforce has done much of the construction work. Continue along the path in front of the imposing lock-side property with its massive flood defence wall. Here we come to Lock 1 and the junction with the River Severn. **Point B.**

The path now ascends a rather steep bank on your left, and onto a smart gravel drive. Follow the drive to the top and you will see a stile on the right leading into a field. Climb the stile and follow the hedge on the right. Between the trees there are fleeting glimpses of the Severn below. At the far end of the field the footpath climbs a slope to another stile. Once over this continue along the right hand side of the field. At the far end are buildings and a high brick wall. At the wall turn right down a bank towards the river, then left over a stile into a meadow. Follow the river bank. Ahead is the handsome Victorian bridge onto Bevere Island, and the huge weir. Boats passing along this stretch head for the other side of the island where a lock is situated. Just beyond the weir we pass through a wooden gate. To the left is a curious long pond in an old watercourse and what looks like a Neolithic long barrow - but it isn't marked as such on the map. Continue along the river bank to another wooden gate. **Point C.**

Don't go through this gate, but turn left along the field hedge. In 100 yards, there is a stile on the right. Negotiate the stile and follow the path ahead to enter a farmyard. After 100 yards, a wooden finger post marks a path off at right angles to the left. Follow the way-mark to a metal gate in the hedge ahead. After going through this gate, keep to the right of the trees ahead, over another stile and along the path by the brook. The path crosses a footbridge, then head slightly to the left of the white house, through a gate and immediately through a gap in the hedge on the right. Once through the next gate, walk slightly to your right towards the furthest tree of the line of trees coming in from the right. Then another stile takes us onto the lane where we turn left. After about 20 yards we take the right fork. Turn right at Bevere House. **Point D.**

We now follow the road past Bevere Vivis Gallery on the left. This is open 10.30-5.00 Tuesday to Sunday in season and is well worth a visit.

At the junction with the main road (the A449) we turn left and after 50 yards turn left again over a stile just before the bus stop. Follow the wooden fence on the right to the far corner of the field where there is a stile hidden until we come right up to it. Once over this we go straight ahead in the direction of a distinctive cedar tree on the skyline, and over another stile. Then keep going straight ahead, still towards the cedar tree and there is a stile right in the far corner of the field. Over this stile and we are back on Lock Lane where the car is parked.

Walk No. 2. Linacre   Distance: 2 miles

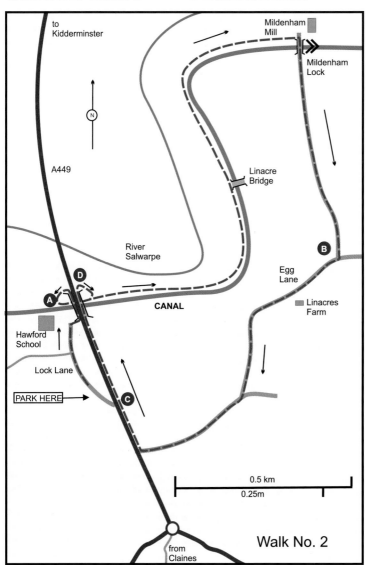

This walk is very easy to describe, as it does not cut across difficult-to-find footpaths. We begin the walk from outside the school at Hawford. To get there from Droitwich, drive south down the A38 towards Worcester, turn off right just beyond the big road bridge after Fernhill Heath (sign-posted to Claines). Go straight on at Claines, then take the second exit off the Northern Link roundabout and head towards Kidderminster on the A449. After a few hundred yards turn off left down Lock Lane (clearly sign-posted) and park on the lane as soon as you find a safe spot.

Leaving the car, continue down the lane towards Hawford School. When the old road stops dead, walk up the path to your right. Turn left and walk along the A449 pavement northwards over the new tunnel. Immediately after crossing the tunnel, turn left down the path into a field. Go through the gate and soon you reach the canal. **Point A.**

Now turn sharply back on yourself to the left and follow the towpath through the new tunnel. Building this tunnel was one of the major pieces of engineering work required to restore the canal.

Now our walk simply follows the towpath for a spell. The route is very pleasantly countrified and we are extremely close to the River Salwarpe in places along this stretch. Please take a moment to examine Linacre Bridge standing in isolation in the fields. It was restored some years ago and looks nicely settled in now. It is one of the few pure Brindley structures on the Canal and is listed.

When we get to Mildenham Lock, we leave the towpath, cross the bridge (which together with the lock is also listed) and head off down the lane away from the mill itself.

We then climb the hill to a road junction where we fork right onto Egg Lane. **Point B.**

Soon we pass Linacres Farm on our left. At the next junction, take the right fork again and continue to the junction with the busy A449. Turn right, and after 300 yards, if there is no traffic, you can cross the road here to reach Lock Lane. **Point C.**

If you wish to avoid having to cross this busy road, you can continue along the verge until you have crossed over the canal. Look for a footpath sign-posted to the right. **Point D.** This leads down to the towpath, and we can re-trace our steps under the tunnel and back to the car.

Walking time approximately one hour.

Linacre Bridge

Walk No. 3. Porters Mill   Distance: 1.5 miles

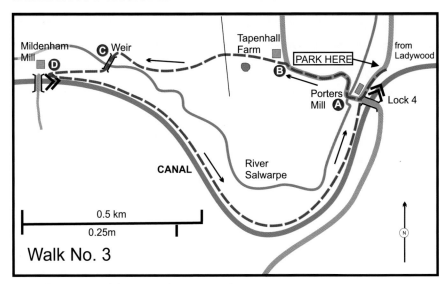

This walk is on part of the Droitwich Barge Canal.

Almost immediately after leaving Droitwich on the A38, heading south towards Worcester. Turn right just before the Copcut Elm pub and first left by the railway bridge, then at the next junction, turn right. Drive on over the canal bridge by Lock Cottage and then fork left and follow the road until it reaches the canal on the left just before Porters Mill. There is usually plenty of space to park here but take care not to obstruct the road or to get stuck in the grass if the ground is wet and soft!

The walk commences along the road to Porters Mill Lock Cottage and at the junction turn right towards Porters Mill itself. **Point A.** The mill buildings are very interesting and all the evidence of the original layout is there to figure out. Why is rushing water so fascinating? I always stop and watch it for a while just beyond the mill where it passes under the road.

Continue along the road for another couple of hundred yards and look out for a footpath to the left through a farm gate just where the road bends and climbs towards Tappenhall Farm up ahead. A finger post marks where the footpath leaves the road. **Point B.**

The path is straight ahead to the right of the pond, then almost dead straight and level across the fields, across a stile to finally follow the bank of the River Salwarpe. As it bends to the left and at this point we cross the river and the mill stream for Mildenham Mill on two footbridges. **Point C.** Another opportunity to stop and watch rushing water!

The footpath then turns to the right between the canal embankment on our left and a boundary hedge on our right. The path ends at the junction of the driveway to Mildenham Mill where we turn hard left onto the towpath back towards Droitwich. **Point D.**

Our walk is now very simple to describe. All we need to do is to follow the towpath back to Porters Mill. This is one of the quietest and prettiest sections of our canal and well worth a walk at any time of the year.

Walk No. 4. Ladywood Locks   Distance: 2 miles

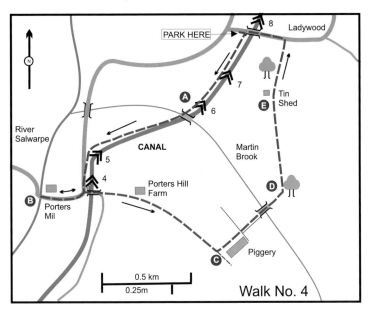

This walk begins at Lock 8 at Ladywood on the Barge Canal. In order to get there drive south out of Droitwich on the A38 Worcester Road. Turn right just before the Copcut Elm pub and first left by the railway bridge, then at the next junction, turn right. At the bottom of the hill the road crosses the canal on a bridge. Park immediately beyond the bridge where it is wide enough to do so, and walk back to the bridge. The walk begins along the towpath on your right heading southwest. After just a few minutes walk we come to Lock 7.

Our walk continues along the towpath past Lock 6, only a few minutes away. **Point A.**

Note the different design of spill weir. Continue along the towpath past Lock 5. Beyond here the canal meets the lane to Porters Mill. Continue to follow the canal by walking on the road side. This idyllic spot comes complete with resident swans.

On the left is an original Brindley Lock Cottage, and behind it Lock 4. But as we come to the road junction turn right and walk down the road a hundred yards to look at Porters Mill itself. **Point B.** As you approach the mill building on your right a mill stream and telltale bricked-in arch at the side of the building show the position of the wheel and its spindle. The top of another wheel can be seen on the other side of the building. It's stream runs under the road to join that of the first. If you study the mill for a while its original layout becomes more obvious.

We must now retrace our steps to Porters Mill lock. The road we are on crosses the canal by an original bridge at the tail of Lock 4. Leaving this tranquil spot, cross the historic bridge and immediately head up a gravel track straight in front of you, which is overhung with trees. This is the Monarch's Way long distance footpath. At the top of the hill we pass Porters Hill Farm (on our left) and continue towards the piggery a quarter of a mile ahead on the left. An overgrown way-mark sign indicates our path to the left just before the piggery. **Point C.** Follow the path with the piggery immediately to your right, through a gate in the hedge to the end of the pig buildings. Then cross the field keeping to the fence, looking out for the wooden bridge over the Martin Brook. Once over the bridge, continue walking ahead to the lone tree in the field. **Point D.** At the tree, turn to your 10 o'clock direction (this sounds like an old treasure map!) and walk toward a large oak tree in a clump of trees. The path goes to the right of the hedge and the metal shed. **Point E.** Ahead should be twin metal farm gates and a stile that brings you onto the lane. Once over this stile turn left and down the lane to where the car is parked.

Before you go take a look at the lock, Lock 8, and you will see the neat Ladywood lock cottage (restored by the Canal Trust) and its garden, wonderful! Please do not trespass on the cottage grounds. The cottage and its gardens are private.

Walk No. 5. Salwarpe   Distance: 2 miles

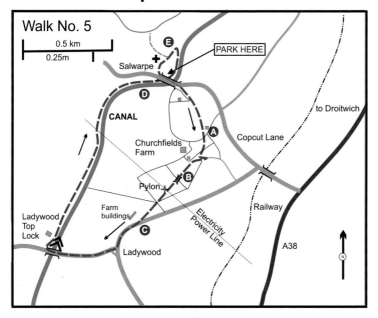

This walk takes in what is probably the best known section of the Droitwich Canals, from Ladywood to Salwarpe. The walk will take about an hour and a half. To begin the walk drive south out of Droitwich on the A38 towards Worcester. Soon after leaving Droitwich turn right just before the Copcut Inn and keep going straight along Copcut Lane to Salwarpe. The best place to park is on the canal bridge just before the church on the right.

Leaving the car, head back up the road a little, and just past the war memorial turn right down an access road. About 20 yards along on the left there is a stile with a way-mark sign (just before The Old Schoolhouse). Follow this fenced-off path to its end then head straight across a field towards a half timbered cottage at the far side. When I did the walk the field was freshly sown with corn, right across the path, but don't worry - you are on a proper footpath. To the right of the half timbered cottage is a gate into the next field. **Point A.**

Now cross the field ahead to a stile about 50 yards to the left of the right hand corner - it is not easy to see until you are nearly upon it. When over, turn to your right and head for a bright galvanised gate. Be sure you secure the gate firmly after you as there are horses in some of these fields. Turn left and walk about 40 yards down the new farm access, then turn right and walk about 40 yards along the concrete access track, where you will see a galvanised gate and a stile on your left. Follow the perimeter fence of the cream cottage on your right. At the corner of the fence, head slightly left and head down the field towards the electricity pylon in the next field. At the bottom of the field, your route is over a small wooden footbridge which is well hidden by trees and the hedge and a little difficult to spot until you are upon it. **Point B.** Once over, keep to the left of the next field, under the power lines and up the rise to the far left corner, where there are two gates at right angles. Climb the stile to the left of the gates and follow the way-mark arrow right and immediately over another stile into a paddock.

Head towards a wooden gate in the little fenced-off section ahead and slightly to your left. Go through this gate and you will see a wooden fingerpost ahead on your left. Go to the fingerpost, climb the stile and cross the plank bridge into the lane. Take care not to step into the ditch which is quite overgrown and invisible! **Point C.**

From here on, the walk is straightforward. Turn right down the lane and after about 400 yards turn right down another lane signposted Porters Mill and Hadley. You will soon arrive at Ladywood Lock. Cross the canal bridge and turn right.

The next section of the walk is back towards Droitwich alongside the canal.

As you come up to Salwarpe, a barn on the left marks the former site of a wharf. **Point D.** From here the towpath has been extensively restored recently. Continue to Salwarpe Bridge. Notice the blue enamel bridge plate '7'. This plate has been used as a prototype for reproduction plates all along the Barge Canal. As you walk ahead along the towpath through the cutting, look up at the top of the bank opposite. The ancient building is Salwarpe Court, here well before the canal was built.

At the far end of Salwarpe cutting, a path doubles back to the church. **Point E.** Take this path and walk up the slope to the churchyard. Walk to the left of the church and through the gate onto the road where you are parked on the left.

Boats Moored in Netherwich basin, Droitwich

Walk No. 6. Coney Meadow   Distance: 1.5 miles

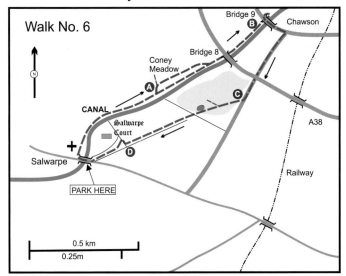

To begin this short walk, drive south out of Droitwich on the A38 towards Worcester. Soon after leaving Droitwich turn right just before the Copcut Inn and keep going straight along Copcut Lane to Salwarpe. The best place to park is on the canal bridge just before the church on the right.

Walk through the church lych gate into the churchyard. Take the gravel path on the right and follow it along the churchyard fence. Passing through a gate ahead, you descend a slope to the canal towpath. Follow this ahead and in a quarter of a mile, you will come to the Coney Meadow Reed Bed. **Point A.** This is a great place to see all sorts of wildlife, which has swiftly become established in this new habitat. There is a picnic bench by the site of the old swing bridge here. If you take the gate off the towpath here into the meadow, you will see the hide ahead of you. By all means take some time here to see what wildlife you can discover in the reeds. You can then either rejoin the towpath and continue to the left, or take the path that runs alongside the towpath hedge. If you do that, then in a third of a mile, you regain the towpath through a wooden gate beneath a large oak tree.

Follow the towpath under the road bridge (Bridge 8) and in a further third of a mile you reach another road bridge (Bridge 9). **Point B.** Pass under this bridge, then immediately turn left up a slope onto the road. Cross the road (with care) and turn left, over the canal. In 50 yards, turn right onto New Chawston Lane. Follow this road for a third of a mile, passing under a road bridge. Do not take the path way-marked immediately after the bridge, but continue a further 150 yards to a way-mark post on the right. **Point C.** Take the track into the wood here, then keep following it as it forks left. When you reach a wooden footbridge over a brook on your left, cross it and continue past a small pond and up a slope. You will emerge into a large field. Your route is ahead of you, but keep to the left hand side of the field by following the hedge. At the end of the field, turn right and you will shortly find a stile in the hedge on your left. **Point D.** A notice now reminds you to keep to the footpath as you are passing through private land. Go over this stile and follow the mown path half left, skirting the hedge ahead as it bends right. You get a great view of the imposing Salwarpe Court (which is not open to the public) before reaching a stile in the hedge ahead. Go over this stile and you are back on the canal bridge where your car is parked.

Walk No. 7. The Junction Canal   Distance: 4 miles

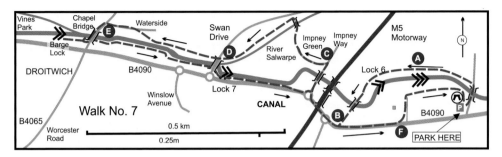

This walk covers all of the new section of canal, with a glimpse of the old line.

For this walk we drive out of Droitwich on the B4090 Hanbury Road, under the motorway bridge. In about 500 yards, turn left into the entrance of the Droitwich Rugby Club, then immediately left again to park at the Pay and Display car park which has a play area and picnic benches.

Leaving the car, make for the wooden steps up over the new canal bridge, then turn left and down the steps onto the towpath. This is the new line on the Junction Canal made necessary due to numerous obstacles on the original route. Follow the towpath towards Droitwich and you will see the new double staircase lock. **Point A.** This is followed by a single lock and up ahead the motorway embankment. As we approach the motorway embankment a footbridge takes us over the canal and onto the pavement of the B4090 where we drove past a while ago. **Point B.**

Turn right towards Droitwich, pass under the Motorway and turn right at the mini-roundabout into Impney Way. You will cross over the canal, then in 100 yards turn left into Impney Green. **Point C.** At the end of this cul-de-sac, take the path that leads beside the River Salwarpe. Turn left and cross over the river on a little bridge, then left again to follow the river. The canal comes in to join the course of the river on your left below the new Lock 7. Cross half-left across Swan Drive, and find where the path continues beside the river. **Point D.** This path emerges onto a residential street, where you turn left and continue to follow the river to a main road. Cross this road with care (watching for traffic), turn left over the canal and join the towpath through a black gate. **Point E.** Your route back is under the road bridge (Chapel Bridge) and along the towpath bordering the newly canalised River Salwarpe.

However, it is worth first diverting to the left to see the Barge Lock, where the Junction Canal and Barge Canal join. Beyond is Vines Park, a pleasant place to spend a few moments to get your breath back.

Passing back under Chapel Bridge, the towpath winds along the bank of the river to emerge, passing under Swan Drive, at Lock 7. Beyond the lock, the towpath diverts onto the road, which you follow to the motorway bridge. After passing under the motorway, continue up the road.

Head up the road towards your car, but keep a very sharp eye open for a somewhat obscured stone milepost in the hedge to your left. **Point F.** This is the start of a footpath which we want to take. Climb through the bushes, and onto the lawn of a big house to your left. Yes this really is a bona-fide footpath. Keep hard up against the evergreen hedge to your right to where it ends. On the right are the ruins of the old Lock 4. The lock itself is partly filled in. Please note that exploring this area is off the right of way, so please keep to the path which goes up the bank and swings to the right. Now head along the footpath through the field parallel with the road you just walked, and over a way-marked stile. The new canal can be seen over to your left. The path is clearly defined and appears to run across private land, but do not worry, this is a public footpath. Finally the path is hemmed in by a 4-rail fence and to the left a stream runs through the trees. This is the Body Brook, which shares the tunnel under the motorway with the new canal! We cross the stream on a wooden bridge and then follow the path to the picnic area where we are parked.

Walk No. 8 Hanbury Locks   Distance: 1 mile

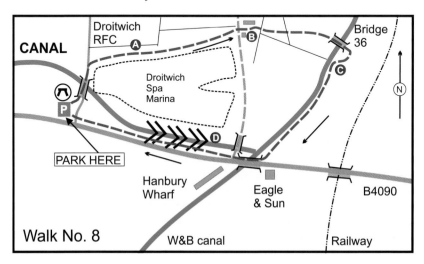

This short walk takes in part of the Worcester and Birmingham Canal and the restored locks at Hanbury Wharf.

For this walk we drive out of Droitwich on the B4090 Hanbury Road, under the motorway bridge. In about 500 yards, turn left into the entrance of the Droitwich Rugby Club, then immediately left again to park at the Pay and Display car park which has a play area and picnic benches.

From the car park, turn left over the canal on the Rugby Club access road and in about 100 yards, there is a small metal gate on the right leading into a field. Go through the gate and then cross the field to the far left corner. **Point A.** This field is the site of the proposed Droitwich Marina. Continue straight ahead across the next field towards a new house at the far side. To the left of the house you will come to a farm road. Walk straight across and down an access track with big modern barns to your left. As the track peters out and swings into the farmyard to your left, you continue ahead into the left hand field, past the way-marked post. **Point B.** When I came this way, I had to negotiate my way around a large dung heap here. Cross the field and look out for a stile directly ahead. The stile has a small footbridge beyond. Once over this, head straight across the next field to where some trees and scrub form a barrier in the middle. Beyond you will see a canal bridge, Bridge 36 on the Worcester and Birmingham Canal. Walk over the bridge, turn right immediately and go through the metal kissing gate leading onto the towpath. **Point C.** Turn left along the towpath. You are now heading south toward Worcester.

After about half a mile along the Worcester and Birmingham Canal we come to a road bridge and just before it the junction with the Droitwich Junction Canal on the right. Leave the towpath here. Go up the ramp, turn right to cross the bridge and then down the access ahead on your right onto the towpath of the Junction Canal. If you peep under the little bridge on your right there is a picnic area set up by volunteers. This raised area was originally at the same level as the towpath to give room for the boater's horses to turn around. However our walk takes us back in the opposite direction, past all the moored boats and the beautifully restored Locks 1 to 3, west in the direction of Droitwich. **Point D.**

Beyond the locks is a short straight stretch of original canal but suddenly the line of the canal veers off to the right. This is the start of the new line, but we follow the towpath and go straight ahead to the Rugby Club road entrance, and our car in the car park alongside.

Walk No. 9. Hanbury Hall   Distance: 5 miles

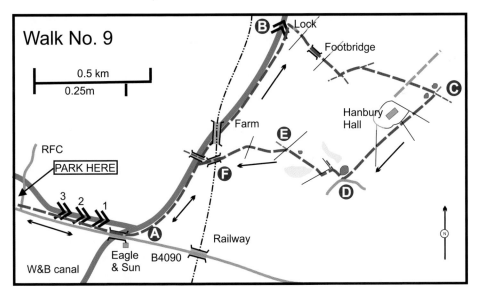

You should allow at least 2 hours to complete this walk.

For this walk we drive out of Droitwich on the B4090 Hanbury Road, under the motorway bridge. In about 500 yards, turn left into the entrance of the Droitwich Rugby Club, then immediately left again to park at the Pay and Display car park which has a play area and picnic benches.

Walk up the wooden steps onto the new canal bridge. From here you can appreciate the new length of canal that sweeps under this bridge. The original line of the canal followed the road down to Droitwich. Cross the Rugby Club access road and descend the steps to join the canal towpath. Follow this to walk away from Droitwich towards the flight of three locks up ahead. Our walk takes us along the Junction Canal past the locks and to the junction with the Worcester and Birmingham Canal (W&B). We then cross the W&B Canal on the main road bridge, turn left and walk down to the towpath on the W&B. **Point A.**

We follow the W&B towpath straight ahead (northwards, towards Birmingham) until we reach the first lock (Astwood Bottom Lock) where we leave the towpath by turning right onto a footpath by the top lock gate. **Point B.** Head straight across the field, a little to the left of a gnarled lone tree, to a footbridge. Once over the bridge, head straight across the meadow to a tall tree where a stile is visible. Follow the way-marked arrow on the stile slightly to the right across a meadow to another stile in a cluster of trees where there is a National Trust sign. Climb over the stile, and turn immediately left over another stile by the National trust sign, then follow the path straight ahead for 90 yards to a footpath signpost.

Follow the way-mark arrow pointing slightly to the right, across the field to a way-marked wooden kissing gate. Continue ahead up the slope. Hanbury Hall and its gardens can be seen on the right. Note the rows of wooden pens protecting the new avenues of trees from nibbling animals! Cross the drive at the top of the hill, continuing straight ahead until the path passes between two small ponds. **Point C.** Immediately beyond the ponds, turn 90 degrees to your right and head towards a gap in the trees with a farm gate and a stile on its left. Climb this stile and walk straight ahead past the entrance to Hanbury Hall. (Why not break your walk with a visit? A cup of tea and a scone in the Refreshment Room is recommended!)

Continuing straight ahead on our walk there is another stile. Once over continue straight on. In this very large meadow is a pine tree and two oak trees up ahead. The path runs a little to the left of the right hand oak tree, and continues straight on to the far side of the meadow where we can see a farm gate and some bushes and trees surrounding a pond.

Head for the gate to the left of the pond, where a stile takes us to the road. **Point D.** At this point take another path sharp right through a gate and around the back of the pond. Ahead is another gate. Go through this and turn right, skirting the field.

At the corner of the field there is a stile but do not cross this one. Our path continues around the edge of the field for about another 200 yards to a gate in the hedge with a wooden footbridge on your right. Cross the footbridge and then walk straight to the right hand corner of a little wood about 150 yards ahead. Now follow the way-mark arrow and head slightly left towards the thickest oak tree in a clump of oaks on the horizon. At the top of the rise, go past a way-mark post on the left of a pond. Continue straight ahead, down the slope and to a metal gate on a farm track. **Point E.**

We now go through this gate, following the way-mark sign for the path that heads to the left away from the farm track and across the field towards a wooden farm gate. Go through the gate and walk ahead along the path on the right hand side of the field towards the bridge over the railway. **Point F.**

Once over the railway bridge walk straight ahead on the path, which brings us to a canal bridge. To the left of the bridge is a metal gate that takes us onto the W&B towpath where we were a little earlier. Go through the gate and turn left (south) onto the towpath. Now all that remains is to retrace our steps to where the car is parked.

The author has taken every care to ensure that the walks are safe and are along permitted paths. Walkers must appreciate there are risks attached to walking down towpaths, through fields and across or down roads. Please take great care, park considerately and follow the country code.

The author does not take any responsibility for accidents, loss, injury or any other misadventure befalling those foolhardy enough to venture out on these walks.

However, I very much hope you enjoy yourself as much as I did and appreciate the beauties of the Droitwich Canals on which so many people worked so hard for so long to bring them back to life.

Salwarpe Court from the canal

INDEX